MYTH, SYMBOL, AND REALITY

BOSTON UNIVERSITY STUDIES IN PHILOSOPHY AND RELIGION

General Editor: Leroy S. Rouner

Volume One

Myth, Symbol, and Reality

Edited by

Alan M. Olson

UNIVERSITY OF NOTRE DAME PRESS
Notre Dame & London

"The Spoken Word and the Work of Interpretation in
American Indian Religion" by Dennis Tedlock is pub-
lished with the permission of the University of Nebraska
Press, which will include a revised version of this essay
in Karl Kroeber, editor, *Traditional Literatures of the
American Indian: Texts and Interpretations* (Lincoln:
University of Nebraska Press, 1981).

Library of Congress Cataloging in Publication Data

Main entry under title:

Myth, symbol, and reality.

  1. Myth—Addresses, essays, lectures.
2. Symbolism—Addresses, essays, lectures.
3. Hermeneutics—Addresses, essays, lectures.
4. Reality—Addresses, essays, lectures. I. Olson,
Alan M.
BL304.M87   291.1'3   80-11617
ISBN 0-268-01346-2

Manufactured in the United States of America

Contents

Foreword

Boston University Studies in Philosophy and Religion is a joint project of the University of Notre Dame Press and the Boston University Institute for Philosophy and Religion. The series will include an annual volume of papers edited from the lecture series of the Institute as well as other occasional volumes dealing with critical issues in the philosophy of religion. In preparation are volumes of essays on transcendence and the sacred and on meaning and truth in nineteenth-century philosophy and religion.

The Boston University Institute for Philosophy and Religion is sponsored jointly by the School of Theology, the Department of Philosophy, the Department of Religion, and the Graduate School of Boston University. As an interdisciplinary and ecumenical forum it does not represent any philosophical school or religious tradition. Within the academic community it is committed to dialogue on questions of value, truth, and ultimate meaning, which transcends the narrow specialization of academic life. Outside the university community it seeks to recover the "public tradition" of philosophical discourse which was a lively part of American intellectual life in the early years of this century, before the professionalization of both philosophy and religious studies.

Our themes are purposely broad and inclusive. Along with analyses of the theme these Studies will regularly include at least two other approaches besides the analytic one. For example, this first volume begins with essays relating autobiography and philosophical commitment. New occasions often teach new duties, and especially with senior thinkers we have encouraged discussion of the events and experiences which shaped their thought. These details lend substance to the abstractions of philosophy and theology and help those of us with limited speculative powers see the relevance of sophisticated reflection to ordinary life.

The Institute also encourages comparative approaches to our themes. We live in a world where cooperation is crucial for survival, yet in Ireland, Iran, India—the list could be interminable—that survival is threatened by religious and ideological conflict. Humane scholarship in world religions makes a small but significant contribution to mutual understanding among the world's various believers.

It is our hope that these volumes may be a resource for critical reflection on fundamental human issues both within the academic community and beyond.

Leroy S. Rouner, Director
Boston University Institute
for Philosophy and Religion

This volume is dedicated to PETER ANTHONY BERTOCCI, Borden Parker Bowne Professor of Philosophy, Emeritus, at Boston University, who has seen his pioneering work with the Institute grow into an ongoing program of research and publication.

Acknowledgments

We wish to acknowledge and to thank all persons involved with the programs of the Institute, especially the lecturers and essayists for their patient cooperation during the preparation of this collection. Special words of appreciation are due to Rebecca Low, James Dutton, and Karol Kelliher for typing and editorial assistance, to Christopher Frost for assisting with the indexing, and, above all, to Gayle Gerber Koontz for primary editorial and technical assistance in the final preparation of the manuscript.

Alan M. Olson

Contributors

J. N. FINDLAY is University Professor and Borden Parker Bowne Professor of Philosophy at Boston University. His books include *Meinong's Theory of Objects* (1933), *Hegel: A Re-Examination* (1958), *Values and Intentions* (1961), *Language, Mind and Value* (1963), *Meinong's Theory of Objects and Values* (1963), *The Discipline of the Cave* (1966), *The Transcendence of the Cave* (1967), *Ascent to the Absolute* (1970), *Axiological Ethics* (1970), *Plato: The Written and Unwritten Doctrines* (1974). He is now working on *Kant and the Transcendental Object*. Mr. Findlay received his B.A. and M.A. at Transvaal University College, South Africa. He was a Rhodes Scholar and received a B.A. First-Class Honours in Literae Humaniores at Balliol College, Oxford; M.A. (Oxford), 1930. He received his doctorate from the University of Graz, Austria, 1933. He is a Fellow of the British Academy and a Fellow of the American Academy of Arts and Sciences.

HANS-GEORG GADAMER was born in 1900 and took his doctorate at the age of twenty-two under Paul Natorp at the University of Marburg. After World War II he was Rector of the University of Leipzig, before resigning to become Professor Philosophy at Frankfort. He eventually succeeded Karl Jaspers as Professor of Philosophy at Heidelberg, where he continues as Professor Emeritus. He is also occasional Visiting Professor of Philosophy at Boston College. Professor Gadamer's early work dealt with Plato's dialectical ethics.

He is best known today for his *Truth and Method* (1975) and
Philosophical Hermeneutics (1976). He is currently writing
a history of the interpretation of Plato.

HOWARD CLARK KEE's most recent books are *Jesus in History*
(1977), *Community of the New Age* (1977), and *Christianity*
(in 'Major Religions of the World' Series, 1979). Mr. Kee
came to Boston University in 1977 from Bryn Mawr College,
where he was Professor and Chairman of the History of Religion. He is currently Professor of New Testament in the Boston University School of Theology and is chairman of studies
in the biblical and historical field in the Graduate School Division of Theological and Religious Studies. Since receiving
his doctorate at Yale he has participated in archaeological
excavation in various Middle Eastern countries and lectured
in universities throughout the United States, Europe, and
the Middle East.

BERNARD J. F. LONERGAN, S. J., was educated at the Gregorian University (Rome), has taught at Montreal, Toronto,
the Gregorian University, Harvard University, and is currently Distinguished Visiting Professor of Theology at Boston College. Fr. Lonergan's writings include *Insight* (1957),
Collection (1967), *Verbum* (1967), *The Subject* (1968), *Doctrinal Pluralism* (1971), *Grace and Freedom in Aquinas*
(1971), *Method in Theology* (1972), *Philosophy of God and
Theology* (1973), and *A Second Collection* (1975). Fr. Lonergan has been the recipient of many honorary degrees and
awards including the Spellman Award and the John Court-
ney Murray Award from the Catholic Theological Society of
America and the Aquinas Medal from the Catholic Philosophical Association.

HERBERT MASON's *Gilgamesh, A Verse Narrative* was nomi-
nated for a National Book Award in 1971. His dramatic nar-

rative *The Death of al-Hallaj* was published recently, and
his translation of Louis Massignon's *La Passion d'al-Hallaj*
will be published in the Bollingen Series in 1980. His novel
Summer Light, based partially on a myth of Merlin, is
scheduled for publication in 1980. Mr. Mason received his
doctorate in Near Eastern languages and literatures from
Harvard and is currently University Professor of Islamic History and Religion at Boston University.

HAROLD H. OLIVER is Professor of New Testament and Theology at Boston University. In 1963–64 he did postdoctoral
studies at the Universities of Tübingen and Basel. In 1971–72
he was Visiting Fellow of the Institute of Theoretical Astron-
omy in Cambridge, England. Mr. Oliver has translated two
works of the Basel theologian Fritz Buri and has written numerous articles in leading biblical journals. Three recent articles on themes relevant to his essay in this volume appeared
in *Zygon: Journal of Religion and Science*, in *Theologische
Zeitschrift*, and in *Sources of Hope*, ed. Ross Fitzgerald. Mr.
Oliver holds a master's degree in theology from Princeton
Seminary and a Ph.D. in liberal arts from Emory University. He has recently been appointed a member of the Editorial Advisory Board of *Zygon*.

ALAN M. OLSON is Program Coordinator of the Boston University Institute for Philosophy and Religion and Assistant Professor of Religion at Boston University. He is the editor of
*Disguises of the Demonic: Contemporary Perspectives on
the Power of Evil* (1975) and the author of *Transcendence
and Hermeneutics* (1979) and of numerous articles and essays. Mr. Olson received his doctorate from Boston University in philosophy of religion and systematic theology. He is
currently coediting *Transcendence and the Sacred: Studies
in Comparative Philosophy of Religion*, the second volume
of Boston University Studies in Philosophy and Religion.

DENNIS TEDLOCK has taught North and Middle American Indian languages, literature, and religion at Iowa State University, Wesleyan University, Yale University, the University of California at Berkeley, and the New School for Social Research. He is currently University Professor and Associate Professor of Anthropology at Boston University. He has done extensive archeological and field research in North and Central America, and is editor of *Alcheringa: Ethnopoetics*, a journal devoted to the translation of tribal and oral poetries. He is the author of *Finding the Center: Narrative Poetry of the Zuni Indians* as well as of numerous articles. With Barbara Tedlock he has edited *Teachings from the American Earth: Indian Religion and Philosophy*. Professor Tedlock received his Ph.D. in anthropology from Tulane University.

JACQUES WAARDENBURG is Reader in Islam and Phenomenology of Religion at the University of Utrecht and the general editor of *Religion and Reason: Method and Theory in the Study and Interpretation of Religion*. His many publications include *L'Islam dans le miroir de l'Occident* (1961), *Les universités dans le monde arabe actuel*, 2 vols. (1966), *Classical Approaches to the Study of Religion*, 2 vols. (1973, 1974), and most recently *Reflections on the Study of Religion* (1978). Professor Waardenburg received his doctorate from the University of Amsterdam and has taught at McGill University and the University of California at Los Angeles.

ELIE WIESEL is the Andrew W. Mellon Professor in the Humanities at Boston University. His seventeen books include novels, essays, stories, portraits, legends, a cantata, plays, and a memoir. Among these are *Night*, *The Town Beyond the Wall*, *The Gates of the Forest*, *The Jews of Silence*, *A Beggar in Jerusalem*, and *Souls on Fire*. *Four Hasidic Masters*, delivered as the ninth annual Ward-Phillips Lectures at the University of Notre Dame, was published in 1978. His two latest works are *A Jew Today* (1978) and the *Trial of God* (1979).

Introduction

ALAN M. OLSON

TAKEN SEPARATELY THE WORDS 'myth', 'symbol', and 'reality' are not particularly perplexing. But when they are placed into a series, as they are in this collection of essays, we are faced with the question of a possible relationship and we have quite a different situation.

That there is a connection between myth and symbol is obvious enough. It is difficult to think of a myth that does not either include symbols or sustain itself upon symbolic or hidden meanings and inferences in one form or another. Conversely, there are many symbols that either are based upon or presuppose familiarity with particular myths. But what about the reality question? Do myths and symbols—and here especially those of a religious nature—have anything at all to tell us about reality? Or do they have to do only with fantastic unreality? Certainly in ordinary discourse the word 'myth' especially tends to be associated and even identified with untruth or falsity, as in the disdainful phrase "Well, that's a myth if ever I heard one!"

Thus, it is precisely with respect to the reality and truth questions that controversy arises, and it is an issue that is by no means resolved—least of all today. Indeed, it is precisely because the question regarding the relationship between the mythic-symbolic and reality has been reopened in our time rather dramatically that we find the occasion for this study. As one of our essayists, Jacques Waardenburg, reminds us, now that the vise-like grip of historicism over scholarship has waned somewhat, it would seem that we are ready for renewed consideration of the

1

reality and truth questions as they pertain to the study of myth and symbol. Many scholars simply do not share any longer the supervening confidence of the positivist-historicist pioneers of the literary-critical sciences in the nineteenth and early twentieth centuries. From George Gershwin's *Porgy and Bess*, the line "It ain't necessarily so . . ."—and scandalous to so many at the time —is rather indicative of the then-fashionable notion that "religion is nothing but a myth." Therefore, against the mood of what Ricoeur terms the "hermeneutics of suspicion" that begins from the position that religion is not what it claims to be, there is now well evidenced the rise of "restorative" hermeneutics.

This is not to suggest that recent scholarship is turning its back on the historical-critical sciences, although in some instances this unfortunately may be the case. It is rather to suggest that much recent scholarship, and certainly the scholarship in this collection, is attempting "to go beyond criticism," as Ricoeur puts it, " by means of criticism." What this means is that one must deploy all the critical tools that are available while not falling victim, in that very deployment, to the new myth of scientism. To put it somewhat differently, while few scholars are willing to deny the blessings of modern criticism, there has also developed a somewhat rival but parallel school of thought that has tried to impress upon us that fact that such so-called blessings are, at best, mixed, especially when they are won at the expense of human enrichment, meaning, and the possibility of self-transcendence.

To focus too long or too strenuously upon what seems to be a kind of loss, of course, would quickly invite the ridicule of being labeled romantic, which such laments quite frequently are. What we present here, by contrast, are the well-reasoned views of scholars from various disciplines who ask that we take myth and symbol seriously. They do not identify what is "really real" with the past, but neither do they restrict it to the present. It is clear, moreover, that the essayists represented here are willing neither to consign the use of the symbolic to the logician and the domain of the value-free mathematical cipher nor to relinquish the mythical to the comparative philologist and anthropologist as something that is "merely of historical interest," as Kierkegaard once put it. The mood of these essays, if I may be so bold, is rather more akin to what Heidegger terms a "retrieval" of meaning through the development of what Ricoeur calls "second" or "post-critical naiveté." To be postcritical, of course, does not mean that one is no longer critical. It has rather to do with striving for that difficult position that is guided by criticism but still open to wonder in the face of what myth and symbol have to give. It is precisely the need for a sense of openness and wonder, I believe, that underlies Jaspers' indictment of Bultmann in the mid-1950s when he argued that what is needed today is not more demythologizing but rather the creative remythologizing of religious meaning. It is a conviction shared by the noted philosopher of science Paul Feyerabend when he recently suggested that no one, not even the scientist, has a privileged vision of reality and that everything—and not just certain subject matter in the humanities—might well be taught under the heading "myth studies."

Thus we do well to remind ourselves that since Jaspers' comment (which is, in many ways, a reckoning point in the study of myth) the meaning of the word 'myth' has moved in its semantic possibilities from univocity to equivocity and even to plurivocity. With the rise of the discipline called mythology we note that the typical dictionary definition of myth became univocal, that is, myth was perceived as having to do with "stories based on ostensibly historical events," but the realities they purport to convey have an "imaginary or unverifiable existence," while mythology has to do with the scientific, that is, "objective," study of such phenomena. But as Heidegger and others have pointed out, the Greek word *mythos* has fundamentally to do with the activity of *telling* and not with the content of that which is told, as though that content could be scrutinized objectively apart from the telling. In a similar vein he tells us in his study of a fragment from Heraclitus that the Greek word *logos*, from which we derive *-ology* as the doctrinal or scientific *word* about something, has as its root the verb *legein* which he describes as meaning "to lay down before in the presence of." Such definitions, needless to say, are highly restorative in their intention, namely, that myth has to do with a telling that seeks to bring the hearer into the *presence* or *region* of that which is told.

We also do well to remind ourselves at the outset that it is peculiar to the nature of religious myths and symbols that one cannot hear or view them neutrally or strictly from the point of view of the spectator. Being or meaning, as Merleau-Ponty insists, "is perspectival," and hence both the myth and the reader or hearer have a *horizon*. If meaning is to emerge then there must take place "the fusion of horizons," as Gadamer puts it, and this fusion is precisely the challenge of hermeneutics and interpretation theory. Therefore, if one is inclined to label something as a myth in the more traditional and frequently perjorative sense, then one can fairly assume that what is deemed mythical is not for that person the object either of veneration or belief and that, in fact, it is quite dead or nearly so. On the other hand, it is highly unlikely that the person for whom a given so-called myth or symbol still displays something significant in the soteriological sense is going to deploy the terms 'myth' and 'symbol' either denotatively or connotatively without severe qualification if they are deployed at all.

What we have described as the movement toward a plurivocal and multivalent understanding of myth and symbol is well illustrated in the first two essays by Herbert Mason and Elie Wiesel under the heading "The Challenge of Myth." In our lead essay Professor Mason argues for what might be termed the invitational or participatory aspect of myth. Quoting William Alfred, he refers to myth as having the capacity to "ambush reality," reality here having to do with what one may think to be really real on the basis of highly limited and restricted vision. As such, certain myths may enable the subject to break free from or at least to extend a very limited horizon through the opening of new vistas of possibility and meaning—even when the myth is archaic and presumed to be prescientific. What Mason describes may be likened to Ricoeur's notion of the "semantic impertinence" of metaphor and the disorienting effect of the parable. Myths and symbols may be impertinent in the sense that they force us to confront meanings and possible realities that are quite foreign to us. As such, they disorient us but not unconstructively, because this disorientation may reorient us to what, in fact, is closer to the truth. When this happens, then semantic impertinence is innovative and has issued in the growth of meaning.

Professor Mason is fond of saying—especially to his students and sometimes but not always as a ruse—"Your problem is that you have not as yet found your myth!" What he means by this, I think, is that life cannot become truly meaningful until it obtains some kind of "emplotment," to use Hayden White's term. In other words, the trouble with most lives is that they suffer from want of an imaginatively productive storyline or plot. For Professor Mason myth (and here especially myths of the epic hero like Gilgamesh) has the power to break us free from the mundane and make us free for new and unknown possibilities of meaning and humanity. Perhaps most importantly of all, Mason insists that myth can provide the occasion for a journey *out* of the self through confrontation with realities *other* than the self. In an age dominated by narcissistic preoccupation with the myth of the self and the plethora of solipsistic intellectual permutations that are its consequence, this is not an insignificant point.

The character of myth and symbol, however, is not always positive. Elie Wiesel reminds us of this very forcefully in his essay "Myth and History," in which he speaks out *for* history and *against* myth as the superior category for the illumination of reality. That Professor Wiesel should do so should not be surprising to the reader familiar with his many literary works dealing with themes of persecution and inhumanity. Indeed, he speaks to us out of a tradition that is especially ambivalent with respect to the meaning of myth, since it has so long suffered under the weight of myths. It is, after all, Christians rather than Jews who have been preoccupied with the meaning of myth insofar as the essence of Christianity is so directly tied to what are sometimes considered to be the mythical dimensions of the work and person of Jesus. One might say that certain aspects of the so-called Christian myth, in fact, are directly at the bottom of the persecution of Jews through the centuries. We simply must not forget that it was the myth of "blood and soil" which, when coupled with the resentment that is characteristic of all forms of bigotry, provided the convoluted rationale for the Holocaust. And one of the more astonishing examples of contemporary mythmaking, as Wiesel indicates, is that in certain quarters people are now denying that the Holocaust ever happened!

Thus against myth and the mythical Professor Wiesel affirms the redemptive character of historical memory unless a given myth is "precisely and clearly defined." The Book of Job for Elie Wiesel has this quality and represents the only truly mythical aspect of Jewish tradition which otherwise is a tradition of law. The reader will be quite taken, I suspect, with this interpretation of Job. The distinction between myth and history, of course, is not so simple as Professor Wiesel first implies. He knows this to be the case by reminding us finally that "the opposite of history is not myth. The opposite of history is forgetfulness."

It is precisely to the problems of differentiating the separate but interrelated domains of myth, symbol, and reality that Fr. Bernard Lonergan directs our attention. While Lonergan assures us that he too appreciates and welcomes the challenge of the mythic-symbolic and its ability to enlarge and enrich our understanding of reality, he also makes it clear that not all myths and symbols can do so equally. In order to receive what it is that myths and symbols give, they have to be interpreted, and acts of interpretation are informed and preformed by the presuppositions, intentions, and values of the interpreter. In other words, the meaning of myth is not immediate but mediated, and it behooves the interpreter to be familiar with the various operations present in the mediational process called interpretation. Lonergan's highly structured position, however, is not to be viewed as being designed for the purpose of imposing upon myth and symbol a positivistic or rationalistic theory of verification. Indeed, it is precisely for the purpose of going beyond the alternatives of a purely analytical versus a purely subjective approach to the meaning of myth that he offers his distinctions concerning the differences between the "infantile" world of immediacy and "being in a world mediated by meaning and motivated by values." Out of this fundamental distinction Lonergan delineates a series of "conversions in understanding," each of which has a bearing on the hermeneutical process. These conversions have to do with the intellectual, moral, and religious dimensions of meaning, respectively: distinctions that turn on a series of dialectical considerations having to do with the relationship between experience and understanding, understanding and judgment, and judgment and personal appropriation or action. The implication of his position is that if one is oblivious either to the separateness or to the final unity of these conversions and their internal operations, and if one thereby confines interpretation to merely one kind of possible meaning (which is so often the case), one will fail to determine the meaning of a given myth or symbol in the most complete possible way.

Fr. Lonergan's allusion to a possible "fourth conversion" that may more completely differentiate the meaning of religious conversion, as evidenced by the recent work of Robert Doran, bears testimony to the fact that his "transcendental method," precise and structured though it may be, is still open and growing. Indeed, it is precisely because, and not in spite, of the care with which Lonergan approaches the mean*ings* of myth that his method can grow, for it is an approach that eschews reductionism in all of its forms at the foundational level through a truly comprehensive cognitional theory. The student of Bernard Lonergan will find particularly helpful, I think, his own narrative account of how this "inductive" system, as he calls it, has developed over the years.

To better orient the reader to the formal study of myth and symbol we begin the next section with an essay by Jacques Waardenburg, whose *Classical Approaches to the Study of Religion* has already become a standard reference in the field. In this essay Professor Waardenburg provides separate analyses of symbol and myth from a multidisciplinary perspective. The student will find his comprehensive bibliography particularly helpful. It is Professor Waardenburg's thesis that the "symbolic aspects of myth" are precisely what underlie the "encounter" and even "confrontation" of the subject with images and realities other than our own, and that through this confrontation there takes place an expansion of meaning concerning the nature of self, world, and the Divine.

Professor Waardenburg, it will be noted, holds in particularly high regard the recent work in hermeneutic phenomenology as an effective way to elucidate the meaning of symbol and myth. Hence we follow his piece with the essay by Harold Oliver in which he advances an adventurous hypothesis having to do with hermeneutics and ontology. This essay attempts to overcome the

apparent gulf between realism and idealism by dissolving both
into what Professor Oliver calls a "relational ontology" that can
far better serve the hermeneutical enterprise. Basic to his thesis is
the notion that the fundamental intentionality of myth is "the imaging of reality as relatedness" and that what is ultimately real in
human experience are "relations" and not entities or *relata*. This
is in sharp contrast to what Professor Oliver sees as the basic assumption of modern philosophy after Descartes, namely, the bifurcation of reality into *res cogitans* and *res extensa* and the
subject-object problem that has dominated epistemology since
Kant. In the modern context what is viewed as being real are the
relata, the subject and the object, the "I" and the "It," with little
attention given to the *between* apart from the thought of Martin
Buber and, according to Oliver, modern physics.

Taking his cue from Buber, physics, and philosophy of science, but also Whitehead, Heidegger, Jaspers, Nishida Kitaro,
Gadamer, and certain mystics like Eckhart, Oliver contends that
what most people regard as being real, namely, entities, are in
fact the "derivatives" of pure experience.

It is Oliver's notion, however, that what we find in myth is
an "imaging" of reality through "re-*present*-ation," and what is
presented is "the announcement of reality [or Truth] as relatedness." The reason that this is the case, he says, is that the originating world of myth is the world of "pure experience as an undifferentiated unity," a notion not far from that of van der Leeuw and
Lucian Levy-Bruhl.

While Hans-Georg Gadamer does not develop at length the
ontological questions that concern Oliver, he clearly resonates to
Oliver's basic approach in saying, "Myth neither requires nor includes any possible verification outside of itself." In Professor
Gadamer's essay, "Religious and Poetical Speaking," he reminds
us, as in the case of Oliver's "alien intentionality," that one of the
basic problems of hermeneutics is recognizing the fact that many
of the questions the interpreter puts to the text are not the questions that the text itself is concerned with. Thus the great challenge, as he puts it, is that of "discovering the question for which
the text is an answer!"

Such a process of discovery is for Gadamer necessarily "dialogical" after the historic model of question and answer. One must become sensitive to the fact, he insists, that this dialogical model is not the same as the "splitting power" that has come to be identified with dialectic after the rise of Greek philosophy. The dialogical approach he envisages has more to do with what we find in Plato's dialogues in which dialectic is identified with the give-and-take of discourse and communication. Indeed, it is precisely the "splitting power" of onto-theology which for Gadamer has given rise to the modern series of "dissociations" between the speaking and what is spoken about, dissociations that arise the moment we assume to be able to know something independently of the event of the "saying."

Professor Gadamer makes it quite clear that within the domain of religion the fundamental dissociation has to do with the separation of worship and faith as we attempt to know the contents of faith independently of worship. However, there is an important difference between poetical and religious texts for Hans Gadamer, especially the New Testament of Christianity. This has to do with the "form" of anonymous address. In the case of the literary text we find an "indeterminate" form of address, whereas the religious text is "determinate" in the sense that its message is to be construed, not as mere information, but as "Truth" for the community of believers.

Paul Ricoeur, more than any other recent theorist, insists that the matter of reference not be abandoned but differentiated. Because of the very considerable impact of his work in hermeneutic phenomenology and philosophy of language I here provide a detailed analysis of those sections of *The Rule of Metaphor* that are of special significance for this study. In this analysis Ricoeur attempts to rehabilitate the entire matter of "sense" and "reference" by focusing on the "split-reference" that is intrinsic to metaphorical predication, and through it he develops what he terms a "tensive theory of metaphorical truth" which aims to do justice to precisely the kinds of speaking that concern Gadamer. In this essay I try to indicate that while Ricoeur is highly indebted to Heidegger and Gadamer, and while he attempts to reconstitute reference as something primarily concerned with meaning rather than object-referral, his analysis also seems to indicate the presence of an as-yet unresolved ontological agenda. This agenda may well reflect the specific problems we have already touched upon concerning the problem of reference in the Gospels, and it will no doubt be one of the primary concerns of his *Poetics of the Will*.

In Part III we present a series of essays dealing with the interpretation of specific myths or complexes of myth. The essay by Dennis Tedlock may be viewed as being responsive to the work of Gadamer, Ricoeur, and Oliver. Indeed, he has found the primary currents of hermeneutic phenomenology and philosophy to be a source of liberation concerning the interpretation of the archaic myths still to be found in oral or quasi-oral cultures like those of North American Indians. In Professor Tedlock's exposition of a Zuni emergence myth he points out that here we are dealing with a world that enjoys, not fixity in the form of a text, but fixity through oral presentation. It is the "telling" of the myth and the phenomena of "stress, pitch, and pause" that bring what is being said into definite shape, form, and meaning. Here again we are informed, this time concretely, that there is an important distinction to be made between a mode of interpretation that is basically dialogical and one that is dialectical. It is Tedlock's assessment that the approach of the ethnologist in the past has been largely dialectical in the dualist sense of trying to fix in a mode of analysis that presupposes reader and text what is, on this model, unfixable.

In the final two essays by Howard Clark Kee and J. N. Findlay we move to a consideration of myths in the written cultures and well-established traditions of the ancient and classical Mediterranean world. Professor Kee, who is of late increasingly preoccupied with the sociology of knowledge as it bears upon the historical reconstruction of early Christianity, here turns his attention to the role of Isis and the impact of this cult on both late Hellenistic Judaism and early Christianity. In this essay we see, rather concretely, the performative power of myth and symbol to shape and condition myths and beliefs of a much larger historical and cultural consequence. The Isis literature is for Professor Kee a perfect illustration of how myths both respond to changing social and political conditions and also themselves become the agents of change. In the earlier and more autonomous period of Egypt's history, he points out, the primary role of Isis was that of being the consort and benefactor of Osiris. But with the rise of Hellenism her role expands from that of a regionally efficacious ordering principle in the Nile and becomes "the rallying point for a mystery cult" that spreads throughout the entire Mediterreanean world. Thus from what some would consider the rather meager origin of being a fertility figure, Isis eventually "assumes a universal significance as the embodiment of wisdom, as the agent of cosmic order, and as the savior of the needy." These transformations are traced through the wisdom literature of Judaism and the *Logos* tradition of the Johannine texts in early Christianity. While to the untrained eye these changes may appear to be rather rapid and dramatic, Professor Kee cautions us that they were in process for hundreds of years as responses to a series of convulsions in the total fabric of ancient and classical Mediterranean culture. What is of great significance, of course, is to have placed before us documentation of how a given myth can leave its permanent mark on subsequent religious and cultural developments that we tend to view as being *sui generis*.

Apart from the controversies surrounding Jesus Christ and mythology, nowhere has more attention been focused than on interpretations of Plato's myths. In his essay Professor J. N. Findlay makes it plain from the outset that he is about to challenge the commonly held assumption that Plato's myths are merely myths. To contend that Plato uses myths simply for the sake of illustration, he suggests, really depends upon what one believes to be ultimately real in the first place. However, since Plato uses myth for the sake of conveying the most sublime truths of morality, how, he asks, can they be viewed as myths at all?

This essay demonstrates again both the impossibility of treating myth and symbol from a position of neutrality and the necessity of a theory of interpretation fully conscious of the processes and operations intrinsic to a conceptual mediation of meaning. Plato was intimately aware of these distinctions, according to Findlay, and for this very reason his strategy regarding myth was akin to that of the mystic philosopher or yogi, namely, the axiological usage of myth for the furtherance of the spiritual education

of humanity. To draw an analogy between Findlay and Lonergan, myth can provide the means of moving understanding beyond sheer immediacy and toward a fuller awareness of what it
means to be in a world "mediated by meaning and motivated by
values." For Findlay the "myths of Plato," therefore, are neither
untruths nor simple illustrations. Myth is rather the instrument
whereby we are effectively moved beyond what is base and tran-
sient in human experience and toward that which is pure and eternal, namely, the values and ideals apart from which life would be
quite meaningless and absurd. Myth can be the bearer of Transcendence. To remove the myths, to cast them aside as being incidental, is akin to saying that we do not need flesh upon our bones.

In summary, it is not the purpose of these essays to pretend
to resolve finally and definitively the meaning of myth, symbol,
and reality, either in themselves or taken as a serial relation. Our
concern is rather "to keep Being's question open," as Heidegger
puts it eloquently, since it is one of the cardinal features of religious myths and symbols to do precisely this.

PART I

The Challenge of Myth

1

Myth as an "Ambush of Reality"

HERBERT MASON

IN OLDEN TIMES A MYTHIC tale depicted the tragedy or comedy of the male[1] will in its confrontations, trials, and journeys to achieve glory for itself, overcome a loss, fulfill a vow, rescue a family, restore an order, outwit an enemy, honor a friend, elude or uncover a truth, search for eternal life, and more. The tales have come down to us in epics, sagas, plays, ballads, poems, incantations, parables, and songs out of an oral historical past that the more incredulous historians find irreducible to meaningful facts, thus unverifiable and irrelevant and, they are inclined to believe, perhaps even nonexistent.

This latter conclusion recalls a friend's encounter many years ago with a French postal clerk in a small town in central France. The friend, an American from Connecticut, had urgently to send a telegram to Boston, Massachusetts, USA. The clerk pulled out one of his comprehensive volumes of international addresses and, after careful search, found Boston, Ohio. He closed the thick book and said definitively, "Boston, Ohio, *oui*; Boston, Massachusetts, *n'existe pas*."

Even from this account of unexpected misplacement we might perceive myth to be, not a mere untruth, but a story rooted in a place where one has been in the past and that one has to reach urgently in the present and that someone at a crucial point on the way says does not exist. It is a story, like most, of facts familiar to oneself but to which, until something happens to make returning to them impossible in the familiar way, one gives almost no thought. Furthermore, it is in a foreign world beyond them that

15

one discovers the possibility of an entirely gratuitous and perplexing challenge to one's assumption about their reality. One is slowly driven to distraction and even almost to doubt of oneself. One may not reach one's increasingly special place in time or at all—Tolstoi's pilgrim does not reach Jerusalem—but by just such a trivial obtuseness one is made to discover within oneself the timeless truth, beyond the facts, of the myth of the desperate journey. Or rather the unfolding myth has discovered oneself in one's innocent panic and disbelief. A myth, as William Alfred has written in the foreword to his modern version of *Agamemnon*, is an "ambush of reality." It hides within the undergrowth of one's ordinary facts, like the voice of Merlin in the whitethorn bush, and seizes an unsuspected reality in oneself.

If one is a poet, by spirit not merely identification with a guild, one's life may be said to begin in just such a moment of being seized. For in the inner distance from reality one begins to see anew what myth reveals—the height one fears, the nearness one loves—without yet knowing why.

A myth—like that of *Gilgamesh*, which may seize especially those who have known loss of a loved one—has a structure, an architecture, a plot consisting of critical dimensions and plausibly changing perspectives. It also has a way of growing within and being completed by oneself; yet it is guided by others previously involved in it from remote times and places who know it as their own. It brings us across such artificial distances as time and space to these others; it translates us from ourselves to them. To some it seems dreamlike and fantastic, though its structure remains orderly through its subtle transformations. Time accelerates and slows, condenses and elongates, just as space envelops and shrinks. We feel together a heightened panic; we experience a more consequential idleness, yearning, and unrest; we grieve more deeply than we did from our private loss.

Instead of leading us on a journey to self, as some believe, it leads us on a journey out of self. We leave the isolation of our perspective and enter the larger, if ultimately limited, universe in which others see what is true to them. The universe is limited, not by others' perspectives, as we feared, but by the structure of creation itself in which we are seized to move beyond ourselves.

Of course, "gliding always near" our seized reality, as Whitman's elegy evokes, is the "dark mother," death, the birth coil of the myth that has ambushed us from without and, inevitably, from within.

The poet must turn even this, especially this, to profit that may not rescue himself but may help others. Indeed, his business from first encounter to last is the knowledge of reality. He embraces this by first studying structure and measure like an architect in service to his myth: through the natural forms and tempi of the life around and within him. For instance, he learns meters from the slow movement of the tree's growth, the quick pulse of the blood's flow, as do the botanist and the physician. Through the unconscious affinities of words found and lost, for instance, in their alliterative attractions to one another and in their disruptive inversions, he learns the way words precede knowledge; and from the conscious assent he gives to their arrangement he learns the sociosyntactical origin of ideas, as does the grammarian. Through space and time expansive and contractive by human and by other forms he learns the relativity of his aspirations and the absolute order of his limitations, as do the mathematician, the astronomer and geographer, and, perhaps above all, the dancer. He in turn teaches in the natural ordered and spontaneous language of life the knowledge of living, timed and timeless, spaced and spaceless, immanent and transcendent; he becomes in turn a transmitter of myth. He knows the dancer's hands are drawn out of his body by a rush of spirit wind; they are not extended there by tight wrists. The dancer and the lover of dance know the difference, though the facts may seem the same, and in the book of facts the wind *n'existe pas*.

The poet through almost blind devotion to his myth knows only existence. The matter of subtle distinctions has already resolved itself in him to obey rather than to engage himself in an ultimately debilitating arrhythmia of private reflections and speculative bibliophilia. He is the true fool of myth, as William Alfred also indicates in his foreword: he knows what he knows.

As may already be obvious from the aforesaid, myth and religion are in deep collusion in this act of ambush. Perhaps they are allied nowhere so naturally as in the *Qur'ān*, where in the chapter

on "the cave" is recounted the tale of obedience of seven young
Christian men who refused to worship a Roman emperor as god
and, with their dog, sealed themselves up in a cave in blind devotion to the will of God. They "slept" for 309 years and then were
"awakened" by God to go forth and bear witness to his truth. As a
dramatic and teaching myth about fidelity this tale seems strikingly different from the critical human need to distinguish between illusion and reality depicted by Plato's cave but not from
its deeper call to the once liberated to return to rescue the still en-
slaved. And the hold each has on its respective civilization and
their generations down to the present day bears witness to the
power of each ambush.

The myth that heralds a call to the heart to be faithful is
rooted in the deepest and highest possible knowledge: of *ma'rifa*
or *gnosis*; not of mere facts, but of transcendent truth. And this
knowledge is not the same as faith: neither the "animal faith"
generalized by Santayana and others nor the formal "religious
faith" particularized by numerous traditions and sects. It is the
knowledge that faith (and indeed even doubt) prepares one for
but can only bring one to its threshold. It is the mythical knowledge to be given, graced, revealed to oneself alone. It is to be uttered in the concrete rhythms one has carefully found in the reality
one did not know existed until it exposed them to the ear. There is
an old Muslim saying: "The heart is a piece of flesh yet a place of
lights." Such sayings accompany old tales and die out only when
one ceases to tell them. The heart, that instrument of love that
confounds itself by tragic imperfection or comic ineptitude, that
confronts its morality with sudden cowardice or odd acts of courage, that is embraced as a rose opening utterly, is embraced by
light. One knows from ordinary facts that in the world of accu-
mulating and competition for wealth, comfort hardens the heart
more than adversity, yet one is not allowed by one's myth of compassion to pray for any heart's suffering.

The heart, which is the desert where the dawn of inspiration
breaks. The arc of the sky, the dwelling place, the house of paradise, the home of quest, where the lord, the guest, comes. The
treasured place the self can effortlessly ruin with a small falseness
in love. The sensual ruby, the pure melted white pearl. The fresh

flowering with varied tints of inspiration, the twists of ecstatic winds, the unfamiliar captive horned animals and flock of rainbow plumed birds. The heart, in the devotion of the truly mad, knows finally that myth is an ambush that brings together, beyond all fears and apprehensions, the lover and the beloved in the deepest and simplest of loves, removing appearances and discrepancies of time and place while reconciling the rich diversity of facts.

In the intertwining worlds of religion and myth, faith like love is a transforming force. The knowledge behind the fiat of each is the Ambusher's to give. The tale remains patiently in wait for the unsuspecting teller to pass by.

NOTE

1. Male, because we have virtually no accouts of female journeyers, warriors, and heroes; and because all accounts to our knowledge were transmitted by men.

2
Myth and History

ELIE WIESEL

I WOULD LIKE TO EXPLORE a personal approach to myth and history, explain why I feel affected by them, tell you a few stories, and then see how we might understand the conflict and the relationship between myth and history in my tradition.

The story has to do with my teacher, who was a Hasidic rabbi, and me. Many years after the war I came to see him in Israel, but by then I had changed. He had not. He still looked like a Hasidic rabbi, but I no longer looked like a Hasid. When I came to him and was properly introduced, he looked at me and suddenly he said, "You are Dodye Feig's grandson." My grandfather was a Hasid. And I said, "Rebbe, I've been working so hard for so many years to make a name for myself, but for you I still remain his grandson."

"But what are you doing?" he asked. "What *were* you doing for so many years?"

"I am writing," I replied. "That's what I'm doing," I said.

"What are you writing?"

I said, "Stories."

"But what kind of stories?"

I said, "Stories."

He said, "True stories?"

I said, "What do you mean, Rebbe?"

He said, "Stories of things that happened?"

And then I caught him. I said, "Rebbe, it's not so simple. Some events happened that are not true. Others are true but did not happen." At that point he was lost. And he simply said, "What a pity."

Myth and history: What are they and how are they related? It is strange that we are suspicious of the first and respectful of the latter, although myths are older than history. Myths precede events, whereas recorded history almost by definition follows them. Myths die, while history does not. In fact, history enjoys the privilege of recording their death. It is unfair, yes. But to say that life is fair is yet another myth. What happens when myths die, and why must they die? Furthermore, where is man's strength? In his ability to create myths or, as in the case of our society today, in his desire to destroy them? "It's only a myth" means it is not serious. "It's history" means it is permanent, triumphant, eternal. We worship facts. The moment you say, "It's a fact," all debate is closed. Fables make us smile. To be vindicated by history is the hope of every great adventurer, politician, and philosopher. Even those who believe in myths for poetic reasons wish to be justified by history. To be called "myth" is derogatory. History as opposed to myth has a clear advantage. History is rooted in the past and at the same time is secure in the future, whereas myth dwells in the past alone, and in the impossible past at that.

In the conflict between the two, therefore, history has been given, somewhat outrageously, the upper hand. The myths of history may appeal to mystics, but the history of the myth will be accepted unanimously as scholarship. As a Jew I must say that our strength has been history and still is, whereas myths have made us weak and vulnerable. We have suffered because of myths, and we have survived thanks to our history. Myths of Jewish power and ambition existed even before there was a Jewish nation. In ancient Egypt, for instance, these myths were handed down from Pharaoh to Antiochus to Hadrian to Torquemada to Hitler to Stalin: the same myths and the same results. Was Jewish blood protected by history? It was not. Jewish life was destroyed and blood was shed because of silly yet dangerous myths that were spread by so many enemies who had nothing in common except their hatred of the Jewish people. They claimed that we killed a god and thus they had to murder *us*. They claimed that we poisoned wells and therefore they had to drown *us*. They claimed that we committed ritual murder and therefore they worked out an elaborate ritual of how to burn Jews. No, we rejected myths. And yet history did not treat us too well either; we have had an ambiguous relationship toward history as well. Often we had reasons to doubt the logic and the justice of history. Occasionally we felt as if history itself were our enemy trying again and again to expel us and erase our imprint.

There is a beautiful story by Chaim Hazaz, an Israeli poet and writer, of a certain Youdke, an innocent fool, almost a simpleton, and yet very wise, who one day wanted to make a speech before the congregation. In front of the assembled worshipers he simply proclaimed his desire to leave history. He wanted to say history was filled with too much Jewish anguish, too many Jewish tears, and too much suffering. He did not want it. He rejected it. Or remember another Jewish writer, André Schwarz-Bart. His hero Ernie Levy, the Last of the Just, wrote to his parents from Marseilles one morning during the war that he had made up his mind to resign from the human race by becoming a dog. For a while he became a dog. How poetic, almost prophetic. If this is the human condition, he does not want it. If this is history, he seeks no part in it. Other nations trust history too much. Not we. And for good reasons. How often have we seen history yield to madness. During the Crusades, for instance, tens of thousands of children, the shepherds, left home one day, moving eastward to Jerusalem, and on the way they massacred and massacred. How often madness has erupted into history. What was the Holocaust one generation ago if not history gone mad?

To oppose myth to history, however, is not correct either, for there is myth in history just as there is history in myth. From a character in a play or novel we can learn much about his author, even more than the other way around. Hamlet has become better known than Shakespeare, and Faust better known than Goethe. Who then is the myth? Paul Valéry said that all myths are linked to language and exist only because of it. What is not said or written about them will remain nothingness. But then history transcends language and progresses without it. You remember events that historians have omitted. What we *can* say about myths is that they are polarized. Some myths are good, others evil. Some commit sin, others do not. In history such lines cannot be drawn. The same people are at the same time, and often for the same motivation, both good *and* evil, capable of sin *and* redemption. Not in myths. Take the myth of the flood, which is a recurring theme in both Judaism and other Babylonian traditions. It is very simple. On the one hand Noah, on the other the wicked. In our own pseudomythology, influenced as it is by other traditions and religions, we have on the one hand Satan, on the other the angels.

Myths as such imply morality or immorality, whereas history calls for objectivity. Myths take sides; history remains neutral. Myths display passion; history is opposed to anything resembling passion. Its only contact with passion is the readiness to record it as it does anything else. We speak of a sense of history, and we try to abide by the so-called laws of history. In the Marxist religion, history attains divine attributes. History never errs and it justifies errors committed in its name. So history has become an implacable force. Its truth is powerful, its power truthful. In other words, it has become personalized. History has created its own gods, its own myth.

What about the Jewish tradition? Are there mythical figures or events in Judaism? My first impulse is to say there are none. We are against myth, against gods. We are against lending too much reality to the myths and too much myth to reality, and therefore we oppose myth. But, after rereading certain texts, I realize I was wrong. There are some mythical figures and events, but not many. Moreover, whenever we encounter a myth, it is presented as such. Whenever we encounter a mythical figure, everything is done to tell us this is not a real figure: it is a myth; the story is invented. Great care is taken to prevent confusion between fact and fable, myth and history, for in Judaism we have learned that the real danger lies not in believing lies but in creating confusion between lie and truth. Take a mythical figure, rooted in reality, Amalek. Amalek symbolizes the archenemy of my people. The law commands any living Jew who meets a living Amalekite to kill that Amalekite. The law is law, but at the same time all measures are adopted by our sages to prevent us from identifying an Amalekite. So he has become myth.

We also have good myths—positive, stimulating, creative, beautiful myths. Take the prophet Elijah, who ascends into heaven but returns forever in disguise. There is the legend of the Thirty-Six Just Men, thanks to whom the world subsides. They are anonymous and must remain anonymous. There is a moral to both. Do not insult a beggar; he may be the prophet Elijah. Do not insult a wanderer; he may be a hidden Just Man. When we deal with myth, we are forewarned. For example, in the Jerusalem Talmud we hear Rabbi Yeoshua ben Levi saying, "Whoever has written this legend will have no share in the world to come, and whoever listens to it will not be rewarded." This total suspicion of legend is countered or balanced by another midrash which praises legends that everyone, not only Jews, will understand, appreciate, study, and communicate.

What does this mean? Like other nations and traditions we need legends and fables to assuage our fears and to stimulate our lives and our fantasy. But we must know they are legends, and they must be treated as legends. Fact must remain fact. For example, the Talmud tells us the strange story of a man who loses his wife but does not have the means to hire a nurse for his infant child. So, he develops two breasts like those of a woman in order to feed the child with his milk. A miracle, says Rabbi Yoseph. "This man must be a saint for a miracle took place because of him." Answers Abbaye, "This man must be a sinner for because of him the order of creation has been disturbed." Obviously the story is a story, not a fact. It is a parable, a fable, nothing else, and *meant* to be a parable and a fable. This is the reason for the exaggeration, the fantasy, and the image. Hence the impossibility of its being real. This brings us to one more legend, and a very beautiful one. Recall the prophet Ezekiel and his famous prophecy when he hears God's voice saying, "Look at these dry bones. One day they will come back to life." In the text, by the way, it is clear this is an allegory. When the people of Israel lose hope, God says, "Do not lose hope. I shall bring you back. I shall open the tombstones and bring you back to the land of Israel." But the Talmud, always a feast of imagination, goes one step further to be sure we take it as legend. In the tractate of Sanhedrin, page 92, Rabbi Eliezer says, "Those who were resurrected by Ezekiel stood up and sang praise to the Lord, but then they died again." The Talmud then begins a discussion about what kind of praise they sang. The next phase. Says Rabbi Yehuda, *Emet mashal haya*, which means, "It was true and a parable." Says Rabbi Nehemiah, *Im emet, lama mashal, veim mashal, lama emet*, which means, "It's either-or." Either it was true or it was a parable. How can it be both? And he himself answers, "It was truly a parable." At this point in the discussion another Master intervenes. Rabbi Eliezer, son of Yosi haglili, decides to push the image one step further. He says, "Oh yes, they were resurrected. Why do you say they died right away? Not only were they resurrected but they came to settle in the land of Israel where they married and had children." At this point still another Master, Rabbi Yehuda ben Betira, stands up and he declares, "Of course, of course they came to Israel, they settled, they married, and I am their descendant. And the *tephilin*, the phylacteries that I am wearing, I inherited from them." It is very clear—the tongue-in-cheek of our Talmudic sages—but what they really mean is "Don't even for a second think this actually happened. A tale is a tale. Facts have to be treated as facts."

There is one mythical character in Judaism—the only one—Job. And the text itself does what it can to tell us immediately that he is mythical.

Once upon a time in a far away and perhaps nonexistent land of Uz there lived a saintly man named Job (a strange name), who had trouble with everybody: with his children who always attended parties, with his friends who added to his suffering, with his wife who gave him unsolicited advice, and with God . . . well, all the rest, forgive me, is theology. The text itself makes the story unreal. Remember the beginning. As a result of a debate, mundane not even theological, between God and Satan, Job is undergoing a series of disasters. He is informed by messengers that the world around him is in ruins. One messenger has hardly left when the other arrives saying, "Your servants were killed and I alone survived to tell the tale." "Your cattle were stolen, the shepherds slain, I alone came to tell the tale." "The house was swept away with the wind and your sons, all of them, are buried there and I alone escaped and came to tell the tale." If you study the text you do not believe it can be a true tale. It is overrehearsed. The messengers all have the same line. There is a stage director. There is an author who told them what to say. If factual, Job's messengers would not repeat so dramatically, so poetically, the same story. Furthermore, why does Job believe them? Why does he not ask for proof, for evidence, for corroboration? How could he think that so many disasters could strike one home, one person, one family, in one afternoon? It is against the laws of chance. Indeed, Job's believing is proof for me that if he existed, Job was not Jewish. Jews do not believe such messengers. Unfortunately in my time, when messengers came to our little town telling us of all the disasters happening to our people, we did not believe them; we thought they were mad. Job believed, but now we do not believe *him*. The story is a story of disbelief. Note the exaggeration even in the midrashic sources: he was a saint of quasi-messianic quality and fiber. He was one of the four men who discovered God by themselves, we are told: Abraham, King Hezekiah, Job, and, mind you, the Messiah.

The book aroused controversy in many quarters for many generations. Some sages distrusted one translation; others distrusted the whole book; and yet . . . on Yom Kippur eve a beautiful ceremony takes place which always makes me weep. On Yom Kippur eve, before the high priest goes the next day to perform his duty in the sanctuary, the ancients of Israel come to spend the night with him, and they study together. The interchange between the old people and the high priest is moving because they want to tell him "Repent." But how can they tell a high priest "Repent"? What kind of sin could he have committed? So they cry because they suspect him; he cries because maybe they are right. They cry because they think they have to teach him; he cries because maybe they are right. So they study. And the book they study that night is the book of Job. Furthermore, we are told in our tradition that had it not been for the tone of the protest, had Job not been too angry with God, we would have included him in our daily prayers. And we would have said: God of Abraham, God of Isaac, God of Jacob, *and* God of Job.

What do we know about Job? Much, too much. So much

that we are confused. When did he live? Once upon a time. But when exactly? Don't ask because you will get more than one answer. Numerous legends make him the contemporary of Noah and Daniel and Ezekiel and Jacob and Moses and Samson and Solomon and the Talmudic sages. Scripture indicates his age as 210 years, but if you take the legends, and you add the years, then he must have lived at least to the age of 800 years. There are also essential facts missing here. We do not know the names of his sons. But, what is worse, neither do we know the name of his father, which in Judaism is rare. We always call ourselves *ben*, "son of"; we must be traced back to our ancestors. We don't know the name of his wife, but we are used to that. Where did he live? Everywhere. Egypt, Canaan, Babylon and naturally Uz, which is a mythical city. His occupation? All occupations. An advisor to Pharaoh, a beloved prince, a just man, a prophet, even a kind of messiah to the Gentiles.

If this were not enough to confuse us, listen to some more hypotheses in the Talmud. There is one in the name of Reb Shmuel ben Nahman who asserts simply and finally, "*Job lo haya velo nivra.*" Job did not exist; he was only a parable. As soon as he has said that, another sage stands up and says, "What? I sat on his grave." Two hypotheses. But then comes a third. The third one says there was a man named Job except he did not suffer. If that is not enough, a fourth one says, "Oh, Job did suffer, but he did not exist." One thing we do know: he did protest. And the protest, of course, is poignant and beautiful. Whenever we try to tell our story, and whenever we try to react to our story, we still use Job. You remember when he asks, "What happened to you, God?" What does he want from God? "How come the wicked are at peace and the just are not? How come," he says, "that the thief in his tent sleeps peacefully, that the killer of the thief is happy, but the victims are not?" Job asks all the questions of theodicy that we have to ask of God, and we are terribly proud of Job. At one point, says the Midrash, more in bewilderment than in sorrow, Job turns to God and says, "Master of the Universe, I do not understand you. Is it possible that you and I are both victims of a case of mistaken identity? Is it conceivable that you confused *Iyov*, which means Job, with *Oyev*, which means the enemy? And that

is why you punished me? You meant someone else?" And strange
as it may seem, of all the questions raised by Job, only this one
was properly answered. God's voice rolled in the tempest: "Pull
yourself together, man, and listen. Many hairs have I created on
the human head, and every single hair has its roots. I do not confuse roots. How could I confuse *Iyov* and *Oyev*? Many drops have
I created in the clouds and every single drop has its own source. I
confuse neither clouds nor drops. How could I confuse *Iyov* and
Oyev? Many thunderbolts have I created, and for each bolt a
path of its own. I do not mistake one bolt for another or one path
for another, how could I confuse *Iyov* and *Oyev*? I have created,"
says God, "the wild goat who is cruel with her young. As the kids
are about to be born, she climbs to the top of a high rock and lets
the little ones drop from the precipice, so I prepared an eagle to
catch them on his wings. But were the eagle to arrive one moment
too early or too late, they would fall to the ground and be
crushed. I do not confuse moments or lightening bolts or drops or
roots, and you ask me if I confuse *Iyov* and *Oyev*?"

Again, strange as it may sound, Job accepts the answer as a
proper answer. Although Job was not Jewish, perhaps God
treated him as a Jew, because he answered Job's question with
another question! To Job's question he says, "*Eifo hayita*, where
were you when I created the winds, when I created the universe?
What do you know about all these matters? What do you know
about justice?" And Job, instead of answering, "Master of the
Universe, leave me with my troubles, the creation of the world is
yours, I want to understand why you punished me, and you
didn't answer me," Job does nothing of the kind. The moment
God says to him "Where were you?" Job repents! Immediately he
tries to atone for his sins, and he says, "Yes, I am guilty, yes, I am
sinful." It makes no sense.

In the beginning I was disillusioned with Job. I felt abandoned; I felt betrayed by him. He, my hero, who should go on
fighting my battle, gives in too soon. But only after I studied and
studied did I realize that even in this episode the authors of the
book did everything they could to make us aware of his mythical
substance, and that he did not give in. Not only didn't he exist,
but he didn't do it—he did not give in. I came to this conclusion

not only in the framework of the relationship of myth and history but when I studied the history of the thirties. Although I was very young, the show trials amazed me, intrigued me, as did the later show trials of 1951–1952. I did not understand the "confessions" of Lenin's companions, great heroes who had the courage to face the jails and the executioners of the czar, who were unafraid, who moved history on their shoulders. Why did they confess? What made them confess? I like to rehabilitate all victims, even these. And I reached the following conclusion. Had they confessed only a little bit, they would have been credible, but they did not. They confessed to everything right away. They did not even argue with the prosecutors. On the contrary, they did whatever they could to blacken their own images. Whenever the prosecutor said, "You are a traitor," they said, "A traitor? An archtraitor. I committed a crime? A hundred crimes." Why did they do it? To create their own myths. To push the very idea of guilt to its grotesque limits. They took a reality and transformed it into myth to make sure we would not believe. And we did not. And we do not.

The same holds true in the story of Job. Had Job argued with God a little bit, had he said, "God, listen, on this point I agree, but on the other I don't," I would have said God won the debate; after all, how can God lose a debate? But Job does not argue. From the beginning to the end we see that he is clear in his mind. The moment God says something he replies, "I'm guilty, I don't argue, I don't discuss, I bow my head," which means he does not bow. I can find in the text another clue to prove my point. At the end, and of course it is a happy Hollywood ending, Job once again marries, again has seven sons, seven daughters, becomes very rich, and at last dies of old age. He dies *zaken u'sva yamim*, which means "happy with life," "full of life." But when you study the text you see that the expression *sva yamim*, which literally means "saturated with years," occurs rarely in our Scripture. In Scripture only one person is described in the same way—not Abraham, not Jacob, and not Moses—but Isaac. Isaac too dies when he is "saturated with years," and this gives us a hint. After his harrowing experience on Mt. Moriah, when Isaac has seen God demand *him* as sacrifice, what pleasure, what joy, what happiness, can he ever again expect to find in life? I think he doesn't. That is why symbolically he becomes blind. He does not find happiness. He becomes a poet. He composes poetry, the Minha-service we are told. When he dies, he is glad, he is very old —"saturated with years"—which means he is fed up with life, and Job is the same. Of course, on the surface Job accepts all God offers him, as if it were possible to replace human life with other human life, children with other children; as if it were possible to compensate for suffering and sorrow. No, Job is "saturated with years." He does not want to live afterwards, but he must, because suicide is not accepted in our tradition.

In conclusion: we are *for* history. We are against myth unless the myth is precisely and clearly defined. Today, in this era, we realize even more than before, the danger of confusing one with the other. I must mention something very concrete which has a meaning for the present. What happened to Job is a prefiguration of what is happening now to my people. One generation ago my people suffered, my people lost its children, my people lost its friends, and my people were abandoned by God. But, at least, there was one possible beginning of consolation—memory or history. Somehow we shall remember, and be remembered.

In recent years an attempt has been made by the enemy, an attempt that is appalling, vicious, ugly. I do not know how to deal with it. I know how to fight injustice but not how to fight vulgarity. There are already sixty-five books in a dozen languages all over the world from Norway to South Africa (imagine the distance and the link), to Germany naturally, to America; sixty-five books all trying to "prove" that the catastrophe did not take place, that Job did not suffer, that the Jewish people did not lose its children and its sages. What do we do about that? I do not know. But one thing I do know: in the Jewish tradition the opposite of history is not myth. The opposite of history is forgetfulness.

3

Reality, Myth, Symbol

BERNARD J. F. LONERGAN, S.J.

I BELIEVE THAT EACH OF the three terms reality, myth, and symbol gives rise to questions. I have no doubt that the questions that are raised are quite different. But I venture to treat all three because in my opinion the style or method of reaching solutions in each case is fundamentally the same.

THE PROBLEM OF REALITY

There arise problems about reality not merely because people make mistakes and even live their lives in error but more radically because they have lived in two worlds without adverting to the fact and grasping its implications. There is the world of immediacy of the infant. There also is the world of the adult, mediated by meaning and motivated by values. The transition from one to the other is a long process involving a succession of stages. We are familiar with the stages: learning to talk, learning to read, learning to write, learning to be good, and so on. But that very familiarity is apt to dissemble the fact that the criteria employed in coming to know the world mediated by meaning and in coming to behave in the world motivated by values are quite novel when contrasted with the more spontaneous criteria that suffice for orienting oneself in the world of immediacy. Samuel Johnson's refutation of Berkeley's acosmic idealism by kicking a stone appealed to a criterion of the world of immediacy but has been thought inefficacious against an elaborate world mediated by

31

meaning. At the same time Berkeley's principle *esse est percipi*, being is being perceived, was an attempt to make the world of immediacy a world mediated by meaning. Hume's radical empiricism was a radical use of the criteria of the world of immediacy to empty out the world mediated by meaning and motivated by values and so revert to the simpler world of immediacy. Kant and the absolute idealists rightly saw that the criteria of the world of immediacy were insufficient to ground a world mediated by meaning and motivated by values. Again, they were right in seeking the further criteria in the spontaneity of the subject. But the worlds they mediated by meaning are not the worlds of common sense, of science, or of history. So I wish to suggest that it is in the immanent criteria of the knowing subject that we may perhaps manage to discover why there are many opinions about reality and even opinions about which is the correct opinion.

Since I am not writing a detective story, let me say briefly what I fancy these immanent criteria to be. A principle may be defined as a first in an ordered set. So there are logical principles, that is, propositions that are first in a deductive process. Again, there are principles that are realities: for example, Aristotle defined a nature as an immanent principle of movement and rest. Now our ability to raise questions is an immanent principle of movement and rest: it is a principle of movement as long as the inquiry continues, and it becomes a principle of rest when a satisfactory answer has been reached. Further, there are three distinct types of question. There are questions for *intelligence* asking what, why, how, what for. There are questions for *reflection* asking whether our answers to the previous type of question are true or false, certain or only probable. Finally, there are questions for *deliberation*, and deliberations are of two kinds: there are the deliberations of the egoist asking what's in it for me or for us; there are also the deliberations of moral people who inquire whether the proposed end is a value, whether it is really and truly worthwhile.

THE PLACE OF MYTH AND SYMBOL

For the rationalist, myth was simply the product of ignorance, if not of waywardness. But a more benign view has been gaining ground in this century. Indeed Plato composed myths, insisting that they were not the truth but gave an inkling into the truth. Aristotle in a later letter confessed that as he grew older he became less a philosopher, a friend of wisdom, and more a friend of myths.

What is the justification of such views? I would suggest that since man's being is being-in-the-world, he cannot rise to his full stature until he knows the world. But there is much that is obscure about the world. People easily enough raise questions for intelligence, for reflection, for deliberation. But we can have hunches that we cannot formulate clearly and exactly, so we tell a story. Stories, as is being currently affirmed, are existential: there are true stories that reveal the life that we are really leading, and there are cover stories that make out our lives to be somewhat better than they are in reality. So stories today and the myths of yesterday suffer from a basic ambiguity. They can bring to light what is truly human. But they can also propagate an apparently naïve view of human aspiration and human destiny.

So we are led from myth to symbols, for there, it would seem, lie the roots of the hunches that myths delineate. But I am not a professional depth psychologist, and so I do no more than direct your attention to the writings of Ira Progoff, specifically to his *Death and Rebirth of Modern Psychology* (1967), which reviews the positions of Freud, Adler, Jung, and Otto Rank, and assigns the laurels to Otto Rank, who for long years was a disciple and collaborator of Freud's but ended with a posthumous work, *Beyond Psychology* (1941), which contended that human destiny is much more than is dreamt of in the worlds of the depth psychologists. There followed Progoff's *Depth Psychology and Modern Man* (1967), which stressed what Bergson would have named the *élan vital*, the formative power that underpins the evolution of atomic elements and compounds, of the genera and species of plant and animal life, of the spontaneous attractions and repulsions of human consciousness that, when followed, produce the charismatic leaders of social groups, the artists who catch and form the spirit of a progressive age, the scientists who chance upon the key paradigms that open new vistas upon world process, the scholars who recapture past human achievement and reconstitute for our contemplation the ongoing march of human history, the saints and mystics who, like the statue of Buddha, place before our eyes the spirit of prayer and adoration, and, I would add, the Christ, the Son of God, whose story is to be read in the Gospels and the significance of that story in the Old Testament and the New Testament.

To conclude this section let me recapitulate. There arise questions about reality, about myth, about symbol. In each case the questions differ. Nonetheless, I would suggest that in each case the style or method of solution is fundamentally the same. It appeals to what has come to be called intentionality analysis. It reduces conflicting views of reality to the very different types of intentionality employed by the infant, the *in-fans* who does not talk, and the adult who lives in a world mediated by meaning and motivated by values. It accounts for the oddity of the myth by arguing that being human is being-in-the-world (*in-der-Welt-sein*), that one can rise to full stature only through full knowledge of the world, that one does not possess that full knowledge and thus makes use of the *élan vital* that, as it guides biological growth and evolution, so too takes the lead in human development and expresses its intimations through the stories it inspires. Symbols, finally, are a more elementary type of story: they are inner or outer events, or a combination of both, that intimate to us at once the kind of being that we are to be and the kind of world in which we become our true selves.

TOWARD FOURFOLD CONVERSION

So far I have been merely outlining my own views on reality, myth, and symbol. But an outline is not a proof, and I may be asked for proof. Unfortunately what proof there is is not deductive but inductive, and the induction is long and difficult. The best I can hope to do is to attempt a Platonic *deuteros plous*, a second best, and tell something of the story by which I arrived at my views.

My fundamental mentor and guide has been John Henry Newman's *Grammar of Assent*. I read that in my third-year philosophy (at least the analytic parts) about five times and found solutions for my problems. I was not at all satisfied with the philosophy that was being taught and found Newman's presentation to be something that fitted in with the way I knew things. It was from that kernel that I went on to different authors.

A first step had already occurred when I was a second-year student of philosophy. I became convinced that universal concepts were grossly overrated, that what really counted was intelligence. At the time I thought myself a nominalist, but a few years later I got beyond that verdict on reading J. A. Stewart's *Plato's Doctrine of Ideas* which contended that for Plato an idea was something like the Cartesian formula for a circle. Obviously that formula, $(x^2 + x^2) = r^2$, is the product of an act of understanding. And I was to elaborate that point later at considerable length in my *Verbum* articles in *Theological Studies*, later published in book form.[1]

A second and related source was Peter Hoenen, a Dutch professor of philosophy in Rome, who during the thirties was writing articles and eventually brought out a book on the nature of geometrical knowledge. I was already familiar with the recurrent lapses from logic in Euclid's *Elements*. But Hoenen was a former pupil of Lorentz of the Lorentz-Einstein transformation and had a far wider range. The example that sticks with me is the Moebius strip. He explained how the strip was constructed, how it was to be cut, how unexpected was the result of the cutting, only to ask whether the result would always be the same when the same procedure was repeated. His answer was a development of the theory of abstraction: just as intellect abstracts universal terms from images, so too it abstracts the universal connection between the universal terms. It was an answer that fitted into the context of Aristotelian logic. But I had shifted somewhat from that context. I believed, not in the abstraction of universals, but in the understanding of particulars and, provided the particulars did not differ significantly, in the generalized formulation of that understanding.

I followed this up in the forties with two historical studies, the first concerned with Aquinas' views on willing, the second with his views on knowing. These labors put my thought in a medieval context. The further labor of transposing it to a contemporary context began when I was invited to give a course on "Thought and Reality" at the Thomas More Institute for Adult Education in Montreal. The Institute was founded at the end of the Second World War in 1945. I lectured one evening a week for two hours. In November forty-five were attending the course. At Easter time forty-one were still coming. Their interest and perseverance assured me that I had a book. Eventually in 1957 it appeared under the title *Insight: A Study of Human Understanding.*[2]

While *Insight* had something to say on evolution and historical process, it did not tackle the problem of critical history. But with this issue I was confronted in its multinational form when I was assigned to a post at the Gregorian in Rome. When I had been a student there in the thirties, the big name in Christology was de Grandmaison, and on the Trinity, Jules Lebreton. Unfortunately, when it became my job to present these doctrines in the fifties, de Grandmaison and Lebreton were regarded as apologists rather than historians. So I found myself with a twofold problem on my hands. I had to extend my theory of knowledge to include an account of critical history, and I then had to adjust my ideas on theology so that critical historians could find themselves at home in contributing to theology. Finally I managed to publish a book on *Method in Theology* in 1972.[3]

More significantly, the book on method has already provided a basis for a distinct advance. In *Insight* and *Method in Theology* I had to develop a doctrine of objectivity that was relevant to a world mediated by meaning and motivated by values. My position was that objectivity was the fruit of authentic subjectivity, and authentic subjectivity was the result of raising and answering all relevant questions for intelligence, for reflection, and for deliberation. Further, while man is capable of authenticity, he also is capable of inauthenticity. Insofar as one is inauthentic, there is needed an about-turn, a conversion—indeed, a threefold conversion: an *intellectual conversion* by which without reserves one enters the world mediated by meaning; a *moral conversion* by which one comes to live in a world motivated by values; and a *religious conversion* when one accepts God's gift of his love bestowed through the Holy Spirit.

The advance to which I wish to allude comes from Robert

Doran of Marquette University. He affirms a fourth conversion. It occurs when we uncover within ourselves the working of our own psyches, the *élan vital*, which according to Ira Progoff has two manifestations. There are the dynatypes and the cognitypes. The cognitypes are symbols. The dynatypes are the root of the life-styles to which we are attracted, in which we excel, with which we find ourselves most easily content. By the dynatypes our vital energies are programmed; by the cognitypes they are released. The spontaneity that has been observed in the hummingbird for the first time building a nest also has its counterpart in us. But in us that counterpart is complemented, transposed, extended by the symbols and stories that mediate between our vital energies and our intelligent, reasonable, responsible lives.

Now it is in the realm of symbols and stories, of what he terms the *imaginal*, that Professor Doran finds a deficiency in my work. With me he would ask: "Why?" "Is that so?" "Is it worthwhile?" But to these three he would add a fourth. It is Heidegger's *Befindlichkeit* taken as the existential question: "How do I feel?" It is not just the question but also each one's intelligent answer, reasonable judgment, responsible acceptance. And on that response I can do no better than refer the reader to Professor Doran's current writing.[4]

NOTES

1. Bernard J. Lonergan, S. J., *Verbum: Word and Idea in Aquinas*, ed. David B. Burrell, C.S.C. (Notre Dame: University of Notre Dame Press, 1967).

2. Now available in paperback from Harper & Row, 1977.

3. *Method in Theology* (New York: Seabury, 1972), and since published in Italian (1975), in Polish (1976), in French (1978).

4. Robert Doran, "Aesthetics and the Opposites," *Thought* 52 (1977): 117–133; "Psychic Conversion," *The Thomist* 41 (April 1977): 200–236; *Subject and Psyche: Ricoeur, Jung, and the Search for the Foundations* (Washington, D.C.: University Press of America, 1977); "Subject, Psyche, and Theology's Foundations," *The Journal of Religion* 57 (1977): 267–287; *Jungian Psychology and Lonergan's Foundations: A Methodological Proposal* (Washington, D.C.: University Press of America, 1979).

PART II

The Study of Symbol and Myth

4

Symbolic Aspects of Myth

JACQUES WAARDENBURG

WITHIN THE BROAD FIELD OF human communication, whether between cultures, communities, or individual persons, the particular signs and stories which we nowadays call symbols and myths have probably always existed. At certain times or moments the symbolic nature of such myths and symbols is felt and understood in a specific way, so that they convey some particular meaning to people in general, but at other periods they appear to be "at rest," apart from their significance for the limited few who feel attached to them and for whom they evoke responses. When symbols and myths have a religious quality, they become points of crystallization because they do not change as quickly as other things with the flux of time but can endure (as points of reference for people) through very long periods of history. In certain cases they can further some historical processes and resist others. But they are doomed to die when they cease to function in the communication between human beings or between an individual and those inner and outer realities which he discovers in the course of his life, for then they no longer play a role in the human quest for sense and meaning.[1]

Although the general theme of this study is that of symbol and myth with regard to reality, we shall refrain here from speaking about the precise nature of the reality to which symbols and myths testify, for there is no certainty that we can reach or speak about that reality at all except precisely by means of such symbols and myths. What we will do is pay attention to people in their capacity as the users of symbols and myths. In phenomenological

41

research we take people's expressions, their witnessing through symbols, myths, and the like, as the only reality we can start from. And if it is the symbols and myths themselves which are the subject matter of research, it is their character as witnesses which is their "reality." We do not need to believe in such symbols or myths, nor do we need to consider them as illusions. It is our task, rather, to try to understand them as they present themselves, namely, as the testimony of people who bear witness to something which has meaning in their historical, social, and human situation.[2]

SYMBOLS[3]

A symbol is more than a sign, since the latter does not imply a representation of the signified. A symbol which is expressed linguistically is also different from a metaphor. Though both have to do with double meaning, the metaphor brings together two dimensions of the same linguistic nature, whereas the symbol brings together a linguistic dimension and another dimension which is of a nonlinguistic nature. Paul Ricoeur, to whom we refer here,[4] adds that in symbols boundaries are blurred for the simple reason that in a symbol different realities meet. This concerns both the boundaries which exist between things and the boundaries which are present between the symbols and ourselves, because to "understand" a symbol implies being involved or becoming involved in it. Unless one stands back again, like a phenomenological analyst first involving and then withdrawing himself, one risks remaining "caught" by the symbol.

Symbolic activity

Most remarkable is the opacity of a symbol, the impenetrability of its symbolic quality which is felt both by the believer or user and by the scholar and philosopher. Ricoeur relates this to the fact that symbolic activity works itself out in different realms of human experience such as dreams, poetic images, and typically religious symbols, which are studied by the different disciplines of psychoanalysis, literary criticism, and phenomenology of religion. Thus there is the problem of coordinating the findings of different disciplines and different kinds of research in order to achieve a more unified and comprehensive understanding of symbolic activity.

Another reason given by Ricoeur for this opacity (at least when the symbolization is verbal) is that we here have to do with a kind of discourse that takes place in the semantic order but that is rooted in a nonsemantic order which imposes itself upon us as an experienced reality and, indeed, precisely as true reality. This nonsemantic order manifests itself in the symbolic experience as powerful and disturbing for a given way of thinking. But at the same time it shows itself efficacious beyond reason, making itself palpable along at least three different lines as "instinct," "mood," and "revealing of the transcendent." These are closely connected and possibly beyond human consciousness. The important point is that humans speak about this kind of reality out of experience and that it is necessary to use symbols in order to speak about it at all. In other words, symbols constitute a special way of expressing oneself about the experience of something which makes itself palpable as a particular kind of reality different from that of daily life subject to ordinary speech.

Involvement and distance

When someone is involved in a particular aspect of reality and expresses himself symbolically, he puts himself at a certain distance from everyday reality and the natural immediacy of the round of activities within which he is used to living and finding himself. The fact that he has arrived at perceiving certain "extraordinary" aspects of ordinary reality will express itself in his response to that reality and in his behavior generally. A pessimistic thinker might say that through the symbol humans alienate themselves from reality and even betray it. There is truth in this insofar as certain symbols can indeed effect an almost total disorientation of people, just as the relevance of old, powerful symbols can be destroyed for most people through a process of conscious brainwashing that also leads to disorientation. An optimistic thinker, by contrast, can interpret perception and the use of symbol as signaling the capacity of the human mind to transcend the mundane world. There is truth in this, too, insofar as the creation or discovery of a symbol very frequently has had a liberating effect on human beings.

A *symbol as instrument of mediation*

If it is true that in a symbol a concrete reality becomes transparent to something else and that a full-fledged symbol implies a transfiguration of a given part of concrete reality, such a symbol should be interpreted then as the bearer of a half-manifest, half-hidden meaning, or as *chiffre* of something which is hidden but palpably working.[5] As soon as the mind is aware of such a transparency, we can speak of a perception of signification, and what the symbol refers to or what it signifies has something to do with the meaning which is in fact perceived. The result is that insofar as meaning has indeed been perceived through the symbol (and in a number of cases the meaning remains unclear or hidden), this meaning extends to the perception of reality at large, to put "ordinary" reality in a different light and reveal different nuances of it.

In most cases we have to do with a more or less "passive" perception of an already existing symbol. Besides the perception of something as a symbol there is also the more active creation and elaboration of a symbol. The person concerned expresses and designates something through the symbol, though he may not be altogether clear himself precisely what is designated. Within a given cultural and religious tradition, however, people will try to identify what is designated in terms of their culture, for instance, as a particular god, power, spirit, demon, or otherwise. Such an interpretation of the symbol, however, takes place after its creation.

It would seem to be more fruitful to account for a symbolic expression within its immediate context and to consider it, for example, as a kind of creative response to an overall situation in which a particular person and a group have been deeply involved. It can then have a harmonious character, revealing the deeper order underlying the situation and suggesting that the given equilibrium should not be disturbed. It can also represent a breakthrough, transcending the self-evident aspects of ordinary reality and the way in which a situation is currently viewed. Such a breakthrough can be painful for the individual and the group involved, though religion can bring a certain relief in at least two respects. On the one hand, such a breakthrough can quickly be identified as religious, since fundamental orientations, attachments, and beliefs are at stake and since there is a serious threat of the annihilation of meaningful existence or even of existence itself. On the other hand, precisely under the threat of such annihilation religion can play an important role by providing an interpretation of the event and reality at large in terms of divine and demonic powers, of revelation and vocation. The result is that symbolic expressions which at first sight are chaotic and utterly confused may lead to mystic vocations and gnostic illuminations, to conversions and new insights into matters of truth and reality.

Whatever may be the cultural or religious interpretation, the creation of symbols, according to the experience of the people concerned, seems always to pass first through a stage of existential oppression and then through a stage of symbolic expression, the result of which is that ordinary reality, both internal and external, becomes bearable again. In a third stage this is articulated in the notion that through the symbol a glimpse of the meaning of life has been perceived. Religious traditions may provide the interpretation that it was a god or divine reality which revealed itself and made ordinary reality bearable for man when he adopted certain attitudes or acted in a certain way. Only on the basis of a careful analysis of the content of the immediate expression can it be concluded whether instinctive fulfillment, artistic inspiration, religious revelation, or something else predominated in the symbolic expression itself or its immediate interpretation. As in the analysis of human expressions in general, the study of symbolic expressions in particular leads to the discovery of basic intentions which underlie any symbolization.

Social/cultural dimension of a symbol

Anthropologists have shown the tremendous importance of the cultural tradition and context in which symbols occur. In order to understand a symbol, these should be thoroughly known since they influence heavily the choice, concrete form, and meaning of symbols and since they throw light on the need for symbolic expression at all in the given circumstances.[6]

Sociologists have stressed that symbols must be generally accepted by a group, community, or society in order to persist and that there must be a certain consensus on their meaning for them to be effective. Such an acceptance and consensus on meaning require a certain authority; religious symbols, for instance, require a religious legitimation supported by charismatic or other authority. All symbols which are recognized by others have a social dimension and function, but they may have more. The code of behavior, especially with regard to religious symbols, tends to be closely related to the values expressed in them, as they are felt by those who are sensitive to them and as they are interpreted by the specialists, even if the actual practice shows great discrepancies with the norms. Consequently, although these symbols strengthen solidarities of different kinds, on closer analysis they turn out to have their own "life" which is closely linked to but not identical with the society's life. There is reason to assume that the real value of the social dimension of symbols is less the solidarity and integration which they bring about for the society than the kind of people produced by the education they provide.

Sensitivity in symbol perception

The cognitive content of symbols has received a great deal of attention, but the way in which this cognition is obtained by the people concerned has been less studied. In particular, religious symbols are often perceived along with more or less profound emotions and powerful physical sensations rather than by means of the analyzing intellect. We have mentioned the pedagogical function of certain symbols, and indeed a gradual development of the personality and the integrative capacities can take place by means of such symbols, provided the individual is sensitive to them. Just as symbols have a social dimension, they have one of sensitivity too, but this dimension is severely threatened in an increasingly rationalized society where intellectual constructions

upon basic "natural" structures and capacities,
them. Old symbols may pass into oblivion here.
and, symbols, once they are perceived and felt, can
an experience of liberation from the ties of the intel-
lec   ie claims of the reasoned word, although in such an ex-
perie   it is symbolization rather than what is symbolized that
predominates.

Religious potentiality in symbols

On the basis of evidence from the history of religions there is
reason to assume both that all symbols can acquire a religious
meaning under certain circumstances or at least show religious
features and also that one particular religious symbol can have
different religious meanings—besides other nonreligious ones—
depending on different religious traditions and contexts. In other
words, any symbolization can develop religious characteristics,
and once a symbol is perceived to be religious it may acquire a
scale of possible meanings. The meaning of a religious symbol,
moreover, can alter in the course of time and be reinterpreted
again and again. The problem is, in fact, how a symbol can transcend its timely birth and continue to exist; religion provides here
a kind of permanency.

It seems important to distinguish among religious symbols
those which may be called "free," because they have not been
codified or canonized religiously by the groups and communities
concerned, and those which may be called "established" religious
symbols within the tradition of constituted religions. One could
speak in the latter case, with Julien Freund,[7] of the sacralization
of such symbols when their forms have been fixed. Just as religious symbolism can be considered as a special case of symbolism
in general, the sacralization of symbols can be seen as a special
process within religious symbolism.

Implicit claims of symbols

As in the case of symbol perception, there seems to be a definite connection between the overall way in which reality is per-

ceived by an individual or a group and a recognition of the
implicit claims of symbols, specifically religious symbols. One extreme is a thorough symbol-blindness linked with the tendency to
view the natural immediate surroundings as the reality, as in the
case with die-hard realists who, for whatever reasons, cannot but
take facts as facts. Another extreme is a spiritualizing tendency to
interpret reality as such symbolically, as in the case with the symbolists who transpose the world, for whatever reasons, into their
own frequently private symbolic universe. A third extreme is to
isolate entirely religious symbols from the ordinary and natural
world and to live, so to speak, in two worlds without much essential connection between them. In such cases the claims of existing
religious symbols are not perceived, and there is no rediscovery or
new interpretation of the religious meaning of a given religious
symbol system.

Hermeneutics of symbols[8]

When in the study of religious symbols we have to do with a
text, we have to start by ascertaining its immediate, literal meaning, and then investigate its immediate sociocultural context. The
same holds true for symbols other than texts. In order to realize
the meaning of *blue* in a given ritual, for instance, we need to
know what meaning the color has in the society in question or for
particular groups within that given society or culture.

A further step is to look systematically into different aspects
of the same symbol. It may contain at the same time a clear pro-
jection of unconscious instincts and wishes, and also the experience of a particular religious meaning with revelatory power. We
simply have to consider the same symbol on different levels, each
one giving access to particular aspects of it. We should simply try
to perceive what dominates in a given symbol without prejudice
as to the inner hierarchy of these levels.

There is also the need to assess the revelatory character of religious symbols as they are perceived and acted upon by the faithful concerned, who view the religious meaning as imposing itself.
As Michel Meslin[9] has put it, the religious function of symbolic
language is to pass from the imagination to ontological reality.

The same holds true for symbols in general, and religious symbols in particular, insofar as they bring about a transposition to another level of reality. This seems to account for the fact that the consciousness changes fundamentally, that given problems, if not solved, at least take on other proportions, and that insights acquired and assimilated lead to new attitudes within everyday reality.

Yet another task is to investigate the geographical and cultural spread of certain symbols and to conduct a search on an empirical basis for a possible common semantic denominator of symbols which are widespread. The problem of the universality of symbolic meanings is of a philosophical nature; comparative studies of symbolism in different times, places, and cultural contexts can bring together important materials for its treatment.

Such a hermeneutic study of religious symbols leads to the hypothesis that a religion consists of a network of symbols which both raises questions of meaning and seems to provide a possible answer, thus making life humanly bearable. They may explicitly reject other possible answers or suggest a certain orientation. Although we are used to speaking of a "religion" only when the meaning offered is guaranteed, so to speak, by a revelation, by a claim of absolute truth, or by a sacralized institution, there is reason to assume that religion is already present wherever such channels of religious meaning are potentially opened up by an effective symbol, before any definite conceptualization or institutionalization.

There remain three kinds of considerations with regard to the interpretation of religious symbols: the general, the sociopolitical, and the philosophical.

First of all, as a general starting point, a religious symbol is an expression of something that is perhaps not at first sight but only in the last analysis considered fundamentally real, like a firm point where one can find an orientation and a truth. Such a symbol can have a definite point of reference, for instance a remembrance, an emotion, an action, or a certain set of words which are more or less fixed and between which one can choose. A symbol can also refer to something indefinite, such as an indeterminate power or reality, or evoke certain more or less arbitrary associations. It can also bypass all determinations and designate some kind of pure transcendence, for instance, through certain sorts of meditation. In these three cases the symbol is conducive to at least three different kinds of experiences. It is exceedingly difficult to find the meanings of a symbol of the second and third kinds of experiences, certainly if one has no personal acquaintance with such experiences. About the third kind of meaning, after all, only personal meditations are possible, but they lend themselves to a certain extent to study. In all three cases a presupposition is that humans have a spiritual dimension that renders them capable of being able to view something symbolically at all and to recognize the symbolic character of a given object.

Second, in the majority of cases there are more or less clear social reasons why certain contents are expressed in a symbolic and possibly religious way, that is to say, concrete social and political realities may prevent immediate expression and make the expression take a symbolic form, mostly as a protest. The "underground" character of certain symbols and the intentions of protest they bear are remarkable. Symbols, moreover, are used by groups in their relations with each other, and consequently they can acquire quite different meanings according to the relationships existing between the groups concerned. The same symbol can be used, for instance, by both the dominating and the dominated party, and it will have opposite meanings accordingly. This mechanism is reinforced and frequently streamlined by the ideologies of the groups concerned, since people adhering to ideologies tend to impose meanings on given symbols from their own vantage-point.

In the third place there are philosophical considerations. The question of the meaning of religious symbols is very much alive now, not only as a question of scholarly research but also as a quest for meaning by many people. Meaning, however, cannot be turned into a pure object nor is it something which can be traded and transferred as a package to supply a need. It is rather to be understood and interpreted, and this is partly a scholarly and partly a philosophical matter. There are at least four philosophical questions which have immediate repercussions for the hermeneutics of religious symbols:

1) Does a symbol, even when its spread and working remain

limited to a particular group or culture, contain a universal feature which enables it to be understood—and even to some extent followed—outside that particular group or culture?

2) How should the life of a symbol be viewed through the various interpretations through which it passes, or the various meanings which are derived from it in the course of time? Certain symbols obtain within specific religions a particular religious meaning: in other cultural contexts they may still be symbols but without a religious reference, while in other circumstances they may simply "cool off" to things without leaving any trace of symbolism.

3) What are the latent and associative aspects of a symbol which distinguish it from other meaning-carriers? The meaning of a symbol is complex and may even manifest a hierarchial pattern; a symbol may be likened to an iceberg in deep water. The problem of latent meanings becomes more complicated if one realizes that a symbol possesses not only more or less objective meanings in a particular culture but also different subjective meanings for different groups and individuals in that culture, given their life experience and expectations, their sensitivities and problems.

4) What can be said of the meaning of a particular symbol in relation to a problem which has not yet fully been identified? If we assume that symbols provide a kind of solution to certain kinds of existential problems, is it possible to recuperate and formulate with any certainty the problem(s) with regard to which a particular symbol has been working?

These four philosophical questions are hermeneutically relevant since within the context of the interpretation of a particular symbol they will influence

1) whether we assume that there is something universal in its content, form, appeal, or symbolic power;

2) whether we concentrate on a few specific—for instance, religious—interpretations of a particular symbol or on all of them;

3) whether we search for the most powerful meaning of a
symbol or also pay attention to other resonant meanings;
4) whether we take the meaning of a symbol to be located in
the possible solution which it offers to a particular problem or in its own autonomous radiation.

Such considerations lead to the conclusion that no interpretations of a religious symbol can be called correct when it does not
take into account all these different aspects: the literal meaning
and the immediate cultural context; the social dimension and the
structural position of the symbol within power relations; the
latent associative aspects connected with feeling and emotion;
some basic philosophical questions, in particular with regard to
the existential problem(s) for which the symbol offers a kind of
solution.

MYTHS[10]

Like symbols, myths were first discovered in connection
with religion, mostly when people were renouncing traditional
religion and beginning to see myths as constitutive for religion. In
the course of time, however, myths like symbols turned out to be
more widespread and not restricted to religion.

We shall make here a basic distinction between explicit
myth on the one hand, as told in the form of a particular kind of
story,[11] and implicit myth on the other hand, as elements in
speech indicating particular and essential assumptions which give
meaning to the life of an individual or community and on which
people can fall back in situations of crisis. Both kinds of myth can
have religious features.

Explicit myth[12]

Several distinctions can be made among the stories of explicit myth, for instance, the division into myths dealing with
gods and other supernatural beings, etiological myths with or
without supernatural beings, myths with a historical basis, and so

on. Attention has been drawn to the historical connection between the origin and development of certain religious myths on
the one hand and the history of certain cults and cult places on
the other hand.

If symbols imply a suspension of immediate reality, this is
still more the case with myths, for what is told in myth seems to
be at an infinite distance from ordinary reality but yet to be relevant for it. In mythical stories reality itself in its various layers of
experience can be put into words, and the interesting thing is that
in myth literally everything can be talked about, so that hidden
aspects and dimensions of human experience, too, can be made
palpable in this way.

An essential feature of these stories in connection with our
theme is that they are of a symbolic nature in the sense that the
story, like a symbol, refers to something that is held to be real and
true. Each element of the myth has to some extent a symbolic
connotation, and the combination of these elements confers a
new symbolic meaning of its own, for the plot itself unfolded in
the story refers to a reality or truth which is represented as an
event of great consequences and implications. These symboliza-
tions together indicate the meaning of the myth, which in most
cases is proclaimed to be a truth upon which the ordinary world
and immediate reality or parts of it are based, so that through the
myth, world and life can be seen in their real nature.

It is characteristic of myth that some profound truth is communicated in the form of a story. Religious myth acquires a kind
of revelatory character through this truth, which reveals something of universal validity about the nature of reality. What is
true is not the details of the story itself but the deeper meanings
which become present to both teller and listener only in the act of
telling. Myths transpose events happening on earth into another
realm of reality where they obtain another meaning, and this
meaning is transmitted back again through ritual plantation.

As in the case of symbols, so also the meaning of myths may
be appropriated in an entirely passive manner. Parallel to the
symbolists who tend to look at everything symbolically are the
mythomanes who tend to see mysteries behind all events, beyond

or within human reach, and who live to some extent in what may be called a mythical universe apart from the ordinary immediate world. On the other hand there are the real creators and elaborators of myth who not only speak at random in mythical terms but are able to convey, in and through mythical story, a precise message in symbolic form which can be translated back into terms of ordinary life. They are the creators of explicit myth.

The relation of myth to history is a complex one. Myths have their own historical development, but conversely they can also be used as an indirect source of historical knowledge.[13] Whereas some scholars, especially in theological circles, have opposed mythical to historical consciousness, others have pointed at the fact that myth reveals precisely human involvement in history. Each myth not only contains the two basic elements of all history, a heroic figure and an event, but also refers, beyond ordinary history, to a kind of absolute history with a beginning and an ending in eternity.

David Bidney, discussing Ernst Cassirer's interpretation of symbol and myth, stresses with Cassirer the need "to analyze the constructive functions of cultural symbols in constituting objective reality."[14] In this vein one may say that myth is a symbolic construction of reality, or a construction of reality by means of symbols. In this connection it is important to notice that the characteristics which we enumerated earlier for the symbol are equally valid for myth, since they stand for its symbolic quality and function: its mediating function, cultural context, social dimension, religious potentiality, implicit claims. Explicit myth expresses an event or action which has a symbolic value, just as a symbol has. But whereas a symbol is of a more static nature, a myth is more dynamic because of its sequence of events or stages, so that it can be called a "moving symbolism," like a film consisting of moving pictures. This dynamic character of myth is also evident from the usual combination of mythical storytelling with symbolic and especially ritual action. Just as one can see in religion a connection between myth and ritual action in cult, so one can see a similar connection between myth and standard-directed action in social life.

Implicit myth

Myths also exist as the meaningful but not fully developed elements of a potential story. Such elements are emotionally loaded and experienced rather than explicitly formulated; the emotions and experiences are often linked with feelings of solidarity between members of a group or between individuals. Mythic elements derive their force precisely from the fact that they suggest rather than explain, and that they constitute cores of meaning without having been put together in a definite pattern. They function as foundation stones for certain basic assumptions in the life of a community or a person.[15]

In nearly all societies, communities, and groups certain symbolic words, actions, or other expressions betray the existence of such mythical elements by which the people symbolically give a "real" foundation to their way of life, legitimating their right of independence, undergirding their struggle for survival, strengthening their desire for fulfillment. As long as these elements remain scattered they may have an immediate appeal, but this will be diffuse and unstructured. But when such implicit myth has become explicit, it has become a story with a sequence of stages and events, and a structure, and hence a more forceful claim concerning the nature of reality. Explicit myth also has a much greater chance to become "officially" religious in the framework of a given religious tradition or system.

In the present time there are certain implicit myths whose elements constitute irreducible cores of meaning with a particular appeal to people. These lead to striking symbolisms which are adhered to beyond critical discourse: particular forms of irreducible dualism, different kinds of absolutized persecution and oppression, liberation and emancipation, various kinds of much desired unity and brotherhood, typical images of longing for paradise on the one hand and of a more or less gloomy future on the other hand. These mythical elements are in our time rarely elaborated into explicit myth; they are rather assimilated in semirational systems called ideologies. The mythical elements betray themselves, however, in any society and culture by their symbolic expression and by the appeal they have to the people; even within an ideology it is precisely the mythical elements which guarantee its appeal. Compared with the elaborate explicit formations of myth in former times, mythical symbolism now seems to grow wild. In addition to the communications media and publicity explosion one can observe today the attempt to make use of symbol and myth by all sorts of diffuse interests. Explicit religious myth outside the world religions is becoming rarer, partly because of the rationalistic tendency to degrade them to the level of folklore and superstition. Implicit myth is more resistent here than explicit myth. On the other hand, new explicit myths can arise now especially as forms of symbolic but real protest which cannot express itself otherwise for political or similar reasons.

Some psychological aspects of myth

This provides an occasion to mention some psychological aspects of myth as well as of symbol. First of all, the appearance of symbols and of implicit myth has something to do with pressures, not only sociopolitical and psychological but also spiritual and possibly religious. The creation of symbol and myth apparently functions as a kind of safety valve against pressure through being able to express something of the truth, if not in a direct then at least in an indirect way. But myth itself, like symbol, can in its turn become oppressive when people are obsessed with one specific myth or are weary of the influence of a particular set of mythical elements. Several possibilities offer themselves as ways of liberation from tired myths:

1) to make out of an implicit myth an explicit one and then to develop a coherent mythology;

2) to assimilate the myth in question to a new myth which has wider claims and possibilities with regard to the interpretation of reality;

3) to denounce myth rationally and straightforwardly as untruth and let *logos* struggle against *mythos*, with the inherent risk that the latter will pop up somewhere else in disguise;

4) to let religion use mythical elements and language with

the claim that it symbolizes another kind of reality than that to which myth refers, in other words, to allegorize myths;

5) to let myth be transcended by persons acting with a view to new aims on their own moral responsibility apart from it.

Of all these possibilities the third seems to be the most interesting from a philosophical point of view. A feeling of oppression by myth itself is already indicative of the fact that such myth is no longer creatively active. As a consequence not only are the powers accounted for in the myth no longer really believed in, but also the power for a mythical assimilation of reality is doubtful. Myth then no longer gives access to reality but rather keeps us away from it. It is largely this feeling of oppression and alienation that explains the uncompromising character of the struggle which reason leads against myth as something essentially "other" in which humans have been caught. If the permanent human task is to interpret reality in such a way that one is able to cope with it, then enlightenment is a permanent human venture as an awakening from mythical consciousness experienced as a burden.

For myth, as in the case of the symbol, the question arises: When can we speak of its becoming religious? For a long time the opinion has been held that those myths are religious which speak of the supernatural and in particular of supernatural beings like gods and demons, insofar as belief in such beings and in a truth connected with them exists. Such a definition of religion on the basis of ideas and representations held is too narrow, however, for at least three reasons: the sheer presence of such ideas of the supernatural does not yet imply religious belief, religious action turns out to be more fundamental and decisive than religious representation, and there are instances of real religion without representations of supernatural beings. Another and more fruitful line of approach is to link religion with the process of absolutization. One can then start with the fact that the symbolization used in a myth can become so strong that not only is the referent of the myth and symbol absolutized but the symbolic instrument itself becomes sacralized and consequently absolutized. This is an indication of the presence of religion.

A *reflective interpretation of myth*[16]

Myth can be understood as a particular form in which humans mentally digest and assimilate reality insofar as it makes itself palpable as an overpowering phenomenon, incapable of being dominated or manipulated completely. Psychological experiences transpose that inner reality through psychic commotions and turbulences which result in dreams, visionary experiences, and reflections at the end of which an insight may arise. In such experiences one feels pressed by reality against the wall of existence or even felled to the ground. Consequently one cannot answer with a real response. However, once a basic structure of the situation has become perceptible, one can begin to sketch the contours of what is slowly becoming conscious. This interpretation accounts for the particular perplexity of being which speaks out of myths and which discharges them into an openness to the wonder of reality and of human being, which is then communicated to others.

Instead of providing such openings to reality, myth can also be made a hindrance to access to reality, surrounding it with nebulousness, hiding it as an inaccessible mystery, and withdrawing it from discussion. Myths that detract from reality can be used to bind people and keep them under control. These are the myths of domination, which imprison people so that they can see and judge reality only in a particular light. Myth here does not open up reality but narrows it down.

Like symbols, myths can appeal to people, even seize them and touch deeper layers in them than those of ordinary experience. It is difficult not to respond to myth, for myths awaken something, certain intentions make themselves valid as a consequence, and certain longings and wishes arise in connection with such intentions. One can speak then of an ethic of myth: good myth and a good use of myth wield a positive influence on people in certain external or spiritual situations; bad myth and a bad use of myth have a negative influence. It is the fruits which witness to the worth of the myths. To a large extent a person becomes a conscious adult because of the cultural "myth heritage" by means of which a living culture transfers a particular kind of education and wisdom to its members. But whereas in nearly all societies such myths as part of culture have had a pedagogical value, in modern Western societies "public" myths tend to be more manipulative since they are produced artifically in the media and advertising and are largely guided by established interests.

Mythology as a beginning of myth-knowledge

The very act of making an implicit myth explicit in the form of a story is a kind of objectification of myth, and so is the act of juxtaposing several myths and putting them into the framework of a more or less reasoned mythology. A *mythology* expresses mythical contents which are contained in different stories within a larger connecting whole. It represents a degree of rationalization of myth and the symbolic message which it is supposed to contain, and it facilitates the transfer of meaning of myth as long as it has not decayed into merely amusing stories. This first objectification is at the same time a first step to a further reasoned knowledge of myth which can basically take two forms.

In the first place such knowledge can place itself and remain within the mythical system itself, trying to understand myth in general or a particular myth on the basis of its own assumptions. Knowledge of myth or mythology in this first meaning is a rationalization of mythical elements which brings these together within an overall framework. For the sake of research or for philosophical reasons it considers myth as conveying a truth which can be recuperated and is still valid. One may speak along these lines of a hermeneutics of myth which runs parallel to what has been said earlier about the hermeneutics of symbolism. In this hermeneutics it is held that myth always contains some truth for whoever cares to listen attentively, but it does not clarify the proportions of that truth, since it is apparently a flash of insight into reality which is reflected upon only later. Hermeneutics, as we shall see, tries to ascertain both the claim of truth of a myth-message and the proportions of the claimed truth.

In the second place the reasoned knowledge of myth can place itself straight outside the myth's assumptions and try to explain it critically on other assumptions. This is, in fact, a kind of unmasking of the myth which may serve to demythologize the truth conveyed by it. There may be a search for its function in an attempt to explain why and how a particular community took a certain myth and used it in a specific context. There may also be an interpretation of the myth from the vantage point of another system, possibly an ideology, a theology, or a wider mythology which is the starting point for the researcher's rationality. There may also be a rationalistic explanation of the myth, intent on showing its particular falsehood or illusory character. The application of such a rationalistic interpretation in practice implies that progress of society is held to demand the full recognition that myths are only myths, that they are to be left as such, and that people should orient themselves in terms of immediate reality on a pragmatical or empirical basis.

Hermeneutics of myth[17]

As with the hermeneutics of symbols, the problem of the hermeneutics of myth is that the very content of what is symbolized cannot be thought out discursively in a completely satisfactory manner. Not without reason has such a discursive consideration been lacking; the contents of myths cannot easily be reduced, desymbolized, or demythologized without being damaged. A simple and natural reaction, bordering on the defensive, on the part of religious people is to consider not only their contents and message but also the symbols and myths themselves as a subject of faith.

The last century and a half has seen a frenetic scholarly search in the West for the meaning of myths. We all know of the basic interpretative schemes which have been applied; myth as figurative wisdom, as a symbolization of nature, as a symbolization of astral constellations, as a structure of society, as a disguised expression of psychic realities, as a revelation of religious truth, as a coded message, as an existential transmission, and so on. Those who undertook the search were historians of religion, anthropologists, sociologists, psychologists, critical rationalists, theologians, often opponents of certain uses to which myth was put. On the whole, however, in their studies they had a positive attitude to myth, which is the more remarkable since precisely this century has witnessed the worst misuses of myth. Notwithstanding the dilettante use and political misuse of myth we can still see it as something worthwhile not only to study but also to listen to. The broad appeal of Mircea Eliade's work on symbol and myth, for instance, gives a clue to the expectations which people have with regard to myth and the force and persistence of myth itself.[18]

Since myth has the form of a story, it seems to be more accessible and can be approached more straightforwardly and naïvely than a symbol. The latter presents itself more clearly as a mystery, and in general people feel that they never understand it completely. For a public accustomed to reading, however, myth seems familiar and can offer itself also as a distraction, a tale. The naïveté, however, consists precisely in believing that it is only a tale and forgetting that it has symbolic meanings which refer to problems which few individuals are able to see and face on their own. It is also easily forgotten that most myths are accompanied by symbolic, often ritual action as a corresponding form of behavior aimed at achieving or maintaining the well-being of a community or individual. What ritual has done to the category of space, diluting it by means of a particular space-bound activity, myth has done to the category of time, widening it by means of a particular time-bound storytelling, and the result is to arouse an awareness going beyond immediate space and time. Our scholarly and philosophical efforts to retrieve certain lost dimensions of myth are little more than an intellectual reconstruction, based on probabilities, with regard to the meaning we are still able to distill from the records of what was once living myth.

In myth research several kinds of meanings of a given myth can be distinguished:

1) the original meaning of the myth when it was made; this meaning is difficult to catch later as it was the symbolic meaning of implicit myth in a bygone situation;

2) the literal meaning of the story with its variants;

3) the place which it has within the total cultural context

within which it appears, and in particular the religious tradition to which it belongs;

4) the social meaning which it has within a given society for different groups and individuals in that society;

5) the message which it contains as uncovered by a formal structural analysis;

6) the different interpretations which have been given of the myth on its own assumptions;

7) the different intentions implied in it and conveyed by it as revealed by a substantial phenomenological analysis. Here the substantial validity and possible universal significance of myth for culture is ascertained, for instance, what it says about being human, about the world, and about truth.

Just as in the hermeneutics of a symbol, the four philosophical questions which were raised earlier also have a clear relevance for the hermeneutics of myth:

1) whether we assume that there is something universal in a myth;

2) whether we search for the most powerful meaning of a myth or also take associative and resonant meanings into account;

3) whether we take the meaning of a myth to be in its proposing a solution to a particular problem, or rather in its ideal radiation;

4) whether we concentrate on a few possible interpretations, for instance, the religious, or on all of them.

The hermeneutics of implicit myth are a still more complex problem since here one has to begin by uncovering a "hidden" myth. This largely comes down to unraveling the implied assumptions or foundation of views with ideological contents and ramifications, which are mostly tabu and kept outside discussion, frequently being viewed as irrational. It is, however, not easy to locate such living, partly hidden implicit myth, to grasp its meaning, context, and implications. But one can try to find the intentions contained in it by taking as a point of departure the appeal of implicit myth to people and the intentions which it evokes in them.

CONCLUSION: SYMBOLIC ASPECTS OF MYTH

It is clear that symbol and myth are again at the foreground of *Religionswissenschaft*. After decades of historical and anthropological research on the facts, there is a return to questions of meaning, with theoretical and philosophical elaborations. There is no need anymore to rehabilitate symbol and myth, and here an attempt has been made only to approach the whole problem anew as a hermeneutical problem: thousands of symbols and myths have been preserved, but what do they mean? Symbols and myths are lying in reserve, as it were. At a given moment a symbol can start working and a mythical element can become active. What kind of reality is then put into motion or is manifesting itself? Both symbol and myth claim to give access to reality, either by particular words, visible objects, and actions or by stories. The superficial judgment that symbol and myth are not real is true only insofar as they are viewed as the simple indicators of reality. But myth and symbol provide access to a reality of a different kind, and the answers they give to problems are not ready-made solutions for well-defined questions but have to do with problems of quite another kind. This has been the subject of the preceding pages.

As we can see clearly at the present time, people are psychologically able to distinguish between those sectors of life which remain open for mythical contents and symbolic meanings and those other sectors where symbolic and mythical interpretations are considered to be illicit or foolish in terms of reason and self-interest. We may assume with some probability that in actual practice the same separation between symbol and myth on the one hand and "practical reason" on the other hand was made in former times too. One field where mythical and symbolic contents were allowed to enter and play a certain role was that which we call nowadays the field of religion, the extension of which has been narrowed in modern society. In many circumstances symbolic actions and mythical representations may accompany daily activities, giving them some sense and perspective, but both levels, although influencing each other, tend to keep to their own logic.

In particular, implicit myth may make people sensitive to existing symbols, whereas explicit myth prefers to use symbols as instruments to convey a message. Conversely, it can be contended that symbols use mythical elements, or *mythologems*, to come to life. In any case there is an immediate relationship between symbols and implicit and explicit myth. Myth as such is a symbolic expression, whereas symbols use mythical elements. The associative and non-delimited character of symbols predisposes them to serve as agents of myth, whereas myth becomes doubly symbolic because it is constructed by means of mythical symbolic elements. The language of symbols and myths within one religious and cultural tradition should, therefore, be basically the same.

It may be contended that myth, like symbol, is born out of the human confrontation with reality and that it expresses both a quest for and a transmission of meaning as a response to this confrontation. A symbol or myth may function, accordingly, as a channel of meaning for people in the particular cultural and religious tradition to which it belongs. Symbolism and the processer of symbolization and myth making are an attempt to integrate symbols and myths into larger wholes and open the possibility of arriving at a reasoned knowledge with regard to reality.

It may be helpful, finally, to evoke an image of the phenomenological analysis of myth, just as the great Levi-Strauss evoked an image of the structural analysis of myth. Whereas Levi-Strauss compares myth to music,[19] I tend to compare the greater myths to painting. Depending on the school of art there may or may not be figures in a painting, but even the greatest nonfigurative art evokes some kind of image within the mind of the observer. Dealing with myth is not merely a matter of listening to an orchestral score. It is rather an encounter, and sometimes even a confrontation, with images explicit or implicit, with other people than ourselves, and with other proportions than our own. When looking at them, we may notice the beginning of an inner dialogue about the life they represent, the world they have made, and the solutions they propose for problems that also confront us, solutions which may be concrete, visible, and direct or less concrete, invisible, and indirect. Interpretations of a painting, and certainly of a portrait, differ widely, and they may come into conflict with each other. But the interesting thing is not so much the conflict of interpretations as the fact that every interpretation deals with the same painting and, evidently, expresses something significant to every attentive observer. So there may also be various ways of viewing myth, but as soon as myth is more than an entertaining story and we enter into its inner dialogue, we can hear the message it has for us which is of universal validity: the *meaning* which it conveys.[20]

NOTES

1. On religious symbol and myth see F. W. Dillistone, ed., *Myth and Symbol* (London: S.P.C.K., 1966) and John Middleton, ed., *Myth and Cosmos: Readings in Mythology and Symbolism* (Garden City, N.Y.: Natural History Press, 1967). See also *International Encyclopedia of the Social Sciences*, 1968 ed., s.v. "Myth and Symbol" by Victor W. Turner. The title of the 1969 Festschrift for Mircea Eliade, *Myths and Symbols* (see note 4), is significant.

2. For the history of myth research see Jan de Vries, *Forschungsgeschichte der Mythologie*, Orbis, vol. 1, no. 7 (Frieburg: Karl Alber, 1961). See also Karl Kerényi, ed., *Die Eröffnung des Zugangs zum Mythos: Ein Lesebuch*, Wege der Forschung, vol. 20 (Darmstadt, West Germany: Wissenschaftliche Buchgesellschaft, 1967). Cf. also Jacques Waardenburg, *Classical Approaches to the Study of Religion: Aims, Methods and Theories of Research: Part 1: Introduction and Anthology*, Religion and Reason, vol. 3 (The Hague: Mouton, 1973) and *Classical Approaches to the Study of Religion: Aims, Methods and Theories of Research: Part 2: Bibliography*, Religion and Reason, vol. 4 (The Hague: Mouton, 1974).

3. See the yearbook *Symbolon: Jahrbuch für Symbolforschung*, 1960 ff., and Jean Chevalier and Alain Gheerbrant, eds., *Dictionnaire des symboles*, 4 vols. (Paris: Seghers and Jupiter, 1973). Besides the work of Mircea Eliade, see Raymond Firth, *Symbols Public and Private* (London: George Allen and Unwin, 1973); Carole E. Hill, ed., *Symbols and Society: Essays on Belief Systems in Action*, Proceedings of the Southern Anthropological Society, no. 9 (Athens, Georgia: Distributed by the University of Georgia Press, 1975); Jacques-É. Menard, ed., *Le symbole*, Colloque international 1974 (Strasburg: Faculté de Théologie Catholique, Université des Sciences Humaines de Strasbourg, 1975);

John Skorupski, *Symbol and Theory: A Philosophical Study of Religion in Social Anthropology* (Cambridge: Cambridge University Press, 1976). See also *Symbolism: Religious, Secular and Social Classes*, Acts of the Fourteenth Congress of the Conference Internationale pour la Sociologie des Religions (C.I.S.R.), Strasbourg, 1977 (Lille, France: C.I.S.R., 1977), and also L. Bryson, L. Finkelstein, H. Hoagland, and R. M. Maciver, eds., *Symbols and Society*, Proceedings of the Fourteenth Symposium of the Conference on Science, Philosophy and Religion, Harvard University, 1954 (New York: Harper and Brothers, 1955).

4. Paul Ricoeur, *Interpretation Theory: Discourse and the Surplus of Meaning* (Fort Worth: Texas Christian University Press, 1976), esp. pp. 53–63. Cf. idem, "The Problem of the Double-Sense as Hermeneutic Problem and as Semantic Problem," in *Myths and Symbols: Studies in Honor of Mircea Eliade*, ed. Joseph M. Kitagawa and Charles H. Long with the collaboration of Jerald C. Brauer and Marshall G. S. Hodgsom (Chicago: University of Chicago Press, 1969), pp. 63–76, and "Parole et Symbole," in Menard, *Le symbole*, pp. 142–161.

5. Michel Meslin, "De l'herméneutique des symboles religieux," in Menard, *Le symbole*, pp. 24–32. Cf. idem, "Pour une théorie du symbolisme religieux," in *Mélanges d'histoire des religions offerts à Henri-Charles Puech* (Paris: Presses Universitaires de France, 1974), pp. 617–624.

6. For a philosophical-anthropological view of the import of symbol and myth see Wilhelm Dupré, *Religion in Primitive Cultures: A Study in Ethnophilosophy*, Religion and Reason, vol. 9 (The Hague: Mouton, 1975). Mary Douglas' work points out the intricate connections between the experience of the body, social experience, and certain types of symbolic construction within some cultures and societies. See *Purity and Danger: An Analysis of Concepts of Pollution and Taboo* (London: Routledge and Kegan Paul, 1966); *Natural Symbols: Explorations in Cosmology* (London: Barrie and Rockcliff; New York: Random House, 1970); *Implicit Meanings: Essays in Anthropology* (London: Routledge and Kegan Paul, 1975).

7. Julien Freund, "Formes et formules," in *Symbolism: Religious, Secular and Social Classes*, pp. 87–104.

8. Cf. Mircea Eliade, "Methodological Remarks on the Study of Religious Symbolism," in *The History of Religions: Essays in Methodology*, ed. Mircea Eliade and Joseph M. Kitagawa, with a preface by Jerald C. Brauer (Chicago: University of Chicago Press, 1959), pp. 86–107. On the hermeneutics of Mircea Eliade see the recent study by Douglas

Allen, *Structure and Creativity in Religion: Hermeneutics in Mircea Eliade's Phenomenology and New Directions*, Religion and Reason, vol. 14 (The Hague: Mouton, 1978).

9. Meslin, "De l'herméneutique," in Menard, *Le symbole*, p. 31.

10. H. W. Haussig, ed., *Wörterbuch der Mythologie* (Stuttgart: Ernst Klett Verlag, n.d.). Besides the work of M. Eliade and C. Lévi-Strauss see Robert A. Georges, ed., *Studies on Mythology* (Homewood, Ill.: Dorsey Press; Nobleton, Ont.: Irwin-Dorsey, 1968); Kerényi, *Die Eröffnung des Zugangs zum Mythos*; G. S. Kirk, *Myth: Its Meaning and Functions in Ancient and Other Cultures* (Cambridge: At the University Press; Berkeley and Los Angeles: University of California Press, 1970); S. N. Kramer, ed., *Mythologies of the Ancient World* (Garden City, N.Y.: Doubleday, 1961); Pierre Maranda, ed., *Mythology* (Baltimore: Penguin Books, 1972); Henry A. Murray, ed. with introduction, *Myth and Mythmaking* (Boston: Beacon Press, 1968); *Mythe en Realiteit: Een cyclus voordrachten gehouden voor de Bilthovense kring voor wijsbergeerte en psychologie* (Amsterdam: Wereldbibliotheek, 1963); Franc Schupp, *Mythos and Religion* (Düsseldorf: Patmos Verlag, 1976); Thomas A Sebeok, ed., *Myth: A Symposium* (Bloomington: Indiana University Press, 1958).

11. "A myth is a type of narrative which seeks to express in imaginative form a belief about man, the world or deity which cannot adequately be expressed in simple propositions," Eric J. Sharpe, *Fifty Key Words: Comparative Religion* (London: Lutterworth Press, 1971), p. 43; cf. pp. 44–45.

12. The division given is of Martin P. Nilsson, who also stressed the link of myths with the history of cults. See his contribution to Gercke-Norden, *Einleitung in die Altertumswissenschaft*, vol. 2, no. 4 (Leipzig, 1931), esp. p. 62 as quoted from Kerényi, *Die Eröffnung des Zugangs zum Mythos*, pp. 223–224.

13. It was J. J. Bachofen who first considered myth, after written texts and archeological findings, as a third class of "monuments" for historical knowledge. See his "Der Mythus als Quelle geschichtlicher Erkenntnis" of 1861, reproduced in Kerényi (See Note 2), pp. 121–123. See also Kerényi's "Wesen und Gegenwärtigkeit des Mythos," in *Die Eröffnung des Zugangs zum Mythos*.

14. David Bidney, "Myth, Symbolism, and Truth," in Sebeok, *Myth: A Symposium*, pp. 3–24. See also Ernst Cassirer, *The Philosophy of Symbolic Forms* (New Haven: Yale University Press, 1955). The original German edition appeared in 1925.

15. It is interesting to observe that Karl Kerényi, one of the great

scholars in the field of Greek mythology in particular, observed that "myth" must have been for the Greeks a kind of fluid mass of data which was brought to life by the art of speaking: *mythologein*. This is similar to what we call the relation between implicit and explicit myth. When we study Greek culture we have to learn, Kerényi observes, not only Greek language but also the materials of mythical nature with which the Greeks thought and expressed themselves; that is to say, we have to familiarize ourselves with their myth as *materia*, as substance. Scholarship has to find ways to let the mythical elements, or *mythologems*, speak for themselves. Kerényi also observes the progressive decay of original myth. See Kerényi, "Was ist Mythologie?" (1939) and "Wesen und Gegenwärtigkeit des Mythos" (1964), in *Die Eröffnung des Zugangs zum Mythos*, pp. 212–233 and 234–252.

    16. See Kees W. Bolle, *The Freedom of Man in Myth* (Nashville, Tenn.: Vanderbilt University Press, 1968).

    17. Cf. Claude Lévi-Strauss, "The Structural Study of Myth," in Sebeok, *Myth: A Symposium*, pp. 81–96.

    18. For the bibliography of Mircea Eliade through 1968 see "Bibliography of Mircea Eliade," in *Myths and Symbols*, ed. Kitagawa and Long, pp. 417–433.

    19. See Lévi-Strauss, "The Structural Study of Myth," p. 88. Kerényi also compares myth with music in *Umgang mit Göttlichem* (Göttingen: Vandenhoeck & Ruprecht, 1955), p. 41.

    20. See also Jacques Waardenburg, *Reflections on the Study of Religion*, Religion and Reason, vol. 15 (The Hague: Mouton, 1978).

5

Relational Ontology and Hermeneutics

HAROLD H. OLIVER

THE CURRENT INTEREST IN hermeneutics owes much to the impetus it received from Martin Heidegger, who determined, in his *opus classicus*, *Being and Time*, that subsequent preoccupation with interpretation would be attended by ontological considerations. The question which informs the entire work stands prominently at the beginning: it is *the question of the meaning of Being*.[1] The terms 'ontology' and 'hermeneutics' in my title betray the influence of Heidegger upon the effort to find an appropriate modern idiom for rendering the classical theme "Being and Meaning." The term 'relational' adumbrates the distinctive thesis to be advanced in this essay.

The theme "Being and Meaning" could in retrospect be said to constitute the haunting philosophical agenda of Western metaphysics. Idealism and realism, with their respective ontologies of the subject-and-object-world, represent alternative readings of the relation of being and thought. Idealism is the historic route of those who place thought prior to being; realism, of those who place being prior to thought. Relational ontology, sympathetic to Hegel's identity of being and thought, conceives being and thought together: being is the presupposition of thought; thought is the articulation of being.

With this introduction the three themes of our presentation have already appeared: ontology, relationality, and hermeneutics. This essay could be construed as an experiment in a new juxtaposing of these fundamental themes.

The dominant role played by epistemology in modern West-

69

ern thought is largely responsible both for the bifurcation of experience into subjects and objects and for the subjectivist bias permeating Western culture. This bifurcation—deeply ingrained into Western philosophy by Descartes—continues to provide much of the dynamic of our modern world and, as a deep and pervasive paradigm, has governed the conceptual choices of millions as to what they have deemed fundamental and of ultimate worth. The extent to which it has served to limit conceptual options should be apparent from the considerable frustration in our culture, a desperation signaling the presence of a troublesome dilemma. Some of the most notable philosophers of our century distinguished themselves by their measured success in suggesting methodologies or paradigms for resolving this dilemma. Phenomenology represents one of the most sustained philosophical efforts to provide an alternative reading of reality. Heidegger sought to move through phenomenology to primal thinking, to that primordial "thinking of Being" conceived as a subjective genitive. Jaspers' periechontology, his ontology of the Encompassing, represented a strongly idiosyncratic systematization of a unifying—as opposed to a bifurcated—vision of reality. Whitehead, the paradigm for all who seek a comprehensive unification of physics and metaphysics, directed his most sustained critique against bifurcationism. The American philosophers James and Peirce exercised sheer Yankee ingenuity to broaden the base of ontology as historically delivered over to America by German Idealism.

In this essay in the relational ontology offered as an alternative to those subjectivist and objectivist ontologies, certain paradigmatic thinkers have provided significant insights. Leibniz stands for all time as the unique alternative to the pervasive but defective ontology entailed in Newtonian physics. Feuerbach struggled desperately to develop his I-Thou model of reality into an adequate relational option to Hegelianism and materialism; neither the Hegelians nor the materialists could be sure whether he was friend or foe. His last major work, *On Spiritualism and Materialism*, exhibits his finest approach to pure relational categories, but, alas, his approach was asymptotic! It was a pupil of the Viennese editor of Feuerbach's collected writings who would succeed where Feuerbach failed. I refer, of course, to Martin Buber, whose philosophy of the "Between" contains those generic notions essential to a fully relational scheme. These thinkers have been my silent mentors, although somewhat after the fact.

Modern physics has been my chief mentor before the fact. Philosophical insights emerging uniquely in the context of theoretical physics, primarily quantum theory and relativity theory, have been most determinative in the development of the relational theory to be set forth in this essay, although in view of the special focus of this essay I shall not rehearse those details here.

A RELATIONAL ONTOLOGY

The term 'ontology' as used in this essay is intended to denote a theory of fundamentals. Ontology—unpopular since Kant— usually evokes images of the transexperiential, thus provoking the charge that it is entirely a speculative business. Kant spoke of ontology as an abyss from which the rational mind can only recoil in terror. Having suggested in the introduction a possible translation of relational theory into the classical idiom of Western metaphysics, I prefer now to keep closely fixed on the notion of experience as articulated by James, Peirce, Nishida, Whitehead, and, to some extent, Bradley. Thus, ontology as used here will mean "a generalized theory of experience." It seeks to proceed from the simplest assumptions about experience, through maximal generalization, to a comprehensive, coherent theory of reality.

If it be objected that all compelling metaphysical schemes have attempted to do the same, a possible response would include the suggestion that other priorities, that is preassumptions, have often intervened to alter the conclusions. Idealistic metaphysics usually proceeds from prior assumptions about the operational priority of epistemology, as I have argued earlier. Realistic metaphysics usually entails prior assumptions derived from uncritical confidence in the *sensus communis*. Process metaphysics, especially as interpreted and defended by Hartshorne and his followers, assumes the fundamentality of asymmetry precisely because of a prior commitment to modal logic, defined by Hartshorne as a "logic of temporality."

Any modern attempt to frame fundamental assumptions can learn much from Kant's choice of questions. The first three of his queries—"What can I know?" "What should I do?" and "What may I hope?"—betray an already bifurcated world: the "I" over against the "known," the "act," "the anticipated." It is clear that the analytic, reflective process has bifurcated the reality it seeks to understand. The first question splits the unitive experience of knowing into knower-known, that is, it introduces a separation, an interval, into the pure act of knowing, with the inevitable result that the "known" is transfigured into a transcendent object, never really available. The second question introduces a temporal interval between intention and act—a common Western error—and so temporalizes the will. The Good becomes a transcendent object, never fully realizable. The third question splits the unitive act of anticipation into the "I" and the transcendent object, "the future," the result being that the future is never really accessible on Kantian terms, as is evident from his mature work *Das Ende aller Dinge*. The presence of the "separated I" in Kant's questions betrays the function of prior assumptions which control the possible answers.

The alternative question suggested by Heidegger, "What is a Thing?" avoids the pitfalls of Kant, that is, unless unreconstructed notions of a "thing" endanger its usefulness. A generalized version of Heidegger's question is to be preferred, namely, what is fundamental, and *eo ipso*, what is derivative? *Fundamental* indicates irreducible features of experience, that is, those features which must enter into every fundamental description. *Derivative* indicates proposed fundamentals that ultimately yield to further generalization.

When this operational question is addressed to experience, the most economical answer—and hence the assumption I make —is that *immediacy* is fundamental. The term 'consciousness'— frequently chosen as the synonym for experience—is rejected as too theory-laden. Thanks to the historic essays of James, Nishida, and Bradley, it becomes appropriate to explicate immediacy in terms of *pure experience*. *Pure* means "prior to reflection," for reflection dichotomizes experience. In reflection the subject is separated from the object. Similarly, methodic doubt splits the unitive act of knowing into knower vs. known. Considering the geometrical proclivities of Descartes, it is not going too far afield to label this result a "spatial" separation. Methodic doubt leads inevitably to the assignment of fundamentality to the *res cogitans*. Moral reflection leads to a comparable dichotomizing of unitive moral experiences, so-called acts of will. Such temporalization of the will separates intention from act, thus transcendentalizing the Good. This phenomenon more than any other, perhaps, has determined the special problematic of Western personhood. I should like to suggest that the supposed fundamentals of Western thought—namely, the Cogito, the subject-self, the Absolute Ego, the Moral Ego, the object, the object-world—are all conceptual products of reflection. They are not fundamental because they are entities of reflected experience, and reflection destroys immediacy.

In pure experience, known intuitively rather than reflectively, there are neither subjects nor objects. There is only experienc*ing*. Since there are no subjects, there is no experienc*er* prior to experienc*ing*; neither is experienc*ing* produced by an experienc*er*. There is neither prior nor posterior. There are no intervals, whether spatial intervals between knower and known or temporal intervals between intention and act. It follows from this characterization of pure experience that immediacy is *pure activity*. Fundamentality inheres in the verbs rather than the nouns, which are usually assigned fundamentality in reflection. The use of the term 'verbs' is problematic in view of the subject-object metaphysics built into Western grammar. Given this fact, it might be best to locate fundamentality through the use of the term 'infinitives.'

The historic connection between subject-object grammar and the theory of relations provides an opportunity to indicate the way in which the appeal to a doctrine of internal relations becomes a defense of reality as immediacy. Position-taking on the doctrine of relations has determined much of the dynamic of Western philosophizing. With no time here to review the modern debate in detail, I can only announce my commitment to the doctrine that all relations are internal, that is, to the view that *relata* are what they are through the relation. G. E. Moore, an opponent of the thesis of universal internality, has given one of the most precise definitions of the thesis underlying strict internality: "any term which does in fact have a particular relational property, could not have existed without having that property."[2] This means formally that apart from prior metaphysical assumptions, given any relation, that is, any *aRb*, *a* is defined by the relation, as is *b*. This claim is the logical opposite of Russell's theory, which assumed that *a* and *b* are "things" entering into relation. And the doctrine of universal internality is a reduction of the views of Moore and Hartshorne, for whom some, though not all, relations are internal. It follows from the simple assumption of internal relationality that *all* relations are fundamental, and *only* relations are fundamental. The *relata* are functions of relating; such functions I call derivatives. Because they are coemergent abstractions, I call them *co-derivatives*. It might be asked whether the claims for the nature of pure experience and the fundamentality of relations are compatible. My conviction is that they are interchangeable variants entailing the same view of reality. It remains to be shown that this is indeed the case. Pure experience is an undifferentiated unity; there are no intervals separating subjects from objects. Thus it follows that space and time, quantitatively considered, are not fundamental, for pure experience is not located in space and time. Immediacy means a now-moment. Space and time can only rightfully be accorded fundamentality to the extent —denied above—that fundamentality can be claimed for subjects and objects. The relational ontology being defended herein asserts, *ex hypothesi*, that relations are not located in space and time. The same claim was made by Leibniz and Whitehead for monads and actual entities, respectively. It is therefore through reflection that the actors (subjects) and the acted upon (objects) emerge. The *ingressive* consideration of a relation results in the notion of "subject," the *effective*, in the notion of "object." These ingressive and effective *co*-operations abstract from the unitive activity, that is, the relating, and hence yield co-derivatives.

What, it may be asked, are the advantages of this paradigm of relation over competing options? I shall mention three: 1) it respects the *given* without disturbing it through reflection, that is, abstraction; 2) it applies one simple principle to the whole of experience; and 3) it does the latter without the reduction necessarily implied in subjectiv*ism* and objectiv*ism*; neither the subject nor the object is absolutized at the expense of the other, for both are accounted for as coaspectual features derived from experience. Hence, idealism and realism are falsified only as *isms*. The category of coderivatives preserves their partial truths while avoiding the debilitating effects that follow when either is made absolute.

I shall now proceed to the presentation of a hermeneutical theory rigorously developed from the relational ontology set forth in the first section of this essay.

A RELATIONAL HERMENEUTICS

Hermeneutics is employed in this second section with the meaning "the theory of the meaning of texts, and of specific statements derived from texts." The texts involved are those belonging to the category of "eminent literature," a term made programmatic by Gadamer. Since my primary focus professionally has been on religious texts, I shall develop the theory with special attention to eminent religious texts. The presentation of the relational theory of interpretation will take the form of a theory of the fundamental *intentionality* of myths, that is, of originative religious texts and *eo ipso* of the statements of belief derived from those texts. This theory will necessarily run counter to rationalistic approaches to these texts which, in my judgment, impose upon them an alien intentionality. Over against the demythologizing of religious texts—popular for a generation—I intend to commend a derationalizing of the hermeneutics of originative religious texts.

It is possible to view the whole demythologizing enterprise—to the extent that it was informed by rationalism—as a struggle not so much with the mythical nature of certain texts as with the modernity of the exegete. The intentionality of myth did not become problematic within mythic experience but from without, namely, from the rationalistic explanation and devaluation of myth. It was precisely the authoritative role of reason in Western culture that generated the kind of critique of myth which—on a relational reading—falls short of understanding. The need for a hermeneutic already signals the loss of mythical-ways-of-being-in-the-world.

The demythologizing debate, which was much broader in scope than Bultmann's historic essay and its aftermath, served to announce the sense of crisis forced upon those within and without religious traditions by the secular ambiance of the last two centuries in the West. At the risk of oversimplifying the issues involved, I propose to thematize what was principally at stake in this debate by affirming the relational intentionality of myth.

The intentionality of myth, referential or relational?

In recent generations of scholarship numerous essays have been written on the intentionality of myth. The lack of a consensus promotes a further inquiry along relational lines.

To the query "What are myths *about?*" the most common answer would probably be that the myths are "stories *about the gods.*" I maintain that within what might be termed prerationalistic mythical consciousness, the questioning ceases at this point except on the defining fringes of mythical cultures. Once that simple naïveté is shattered, the old answer ceases to be adequate both for those who continue within a given religious tradition and for those who define themselves out. Thus, the original question requires reformulation: "What are the stories of the gods *about?*" It was this query, first raised by the Greek Allegorists, that emptied the Olympian Pantheon, for the Allegorists, usually judged uncritical by modern standards, were the first to exercise critical judgment to determine the truth-function of mythical discourse. Prior to that critique the word 'myth' meant simply word or story, without the later connotation of fiction.

The insidious effect of the rationalistic demotion of myth is that it not only defines the stance of those no longer sympathetic with the myths but alters the position of those continuing within those respective religious traditions as well. Reason's sovereignty is absolute; for the *differentiae* it introduces alter consciousness so fundamentally that both those within and those without come to assume the same intentionality of myth, namely, that the stories primarily *intend* to *refer* to transcendent beings. Those within the tradition assert that the referential claims are true, while those without assert that they are false, or more cautiously, non-verifiable. The significant fact for us is, not their respective counterclaims, but the implicit agreement that myths are to be understood *referentially*.

The referential theory of myth has no analogue within the undifferentiated mythical consciousness, for it is a product of rational judgement. In the relational theory of originative religious stories to be set forth presently, the traditional word 'myth' will be used with the single meaning "stories of the gods" and the term 'intentionality' will refer to the primary function of such stories within prereflective mythic consciousness. The relational theory of myth entails the negation of the referential theory, based on the judgment that the latter is grounded in a subject-object paradigm of reality. Such a judgment assumes that a different ontology will issue in a hermeneutics of myth consonant with its assumptions about reality. Fundamental to the relational ontology already presented is the attendant hermeneutical principle that myth is to be interpreted *relationally*.

The intentionality of myth as the imaging of reality as relatedness

This claim will to some appear a bold assertion, partly because to them it may seem to run counter to conventional notions of both myth and reality, and partly because it may seem that a reduction of the intention of myth is thereby effected. In order to justify the relational claim under consideration, I shall return to the simple definition of myths as "stories of the gods." The component "of the gods" indicates what the stories are about *within* what Ricoeur calls the first naïveté. Although the narratives portray actions of divine beings, the originative religious stories give no attention to their reality *per se*. That is not an oversight. The myth is a closed world; no one steps out of it to supplement the narrative. This fact leads us to consider the literary phenomenality of myths, namely, that they are *stories*. As such, understanding what they *tell* is understanding all they *intend*. A story is both *disclosure* and *limit*. What it intends, it conveys; what it does not convey, it does not intend. The task of the interpreter is solely to understand what it intends and to respect what it does not intend. I argued earlier that the referential theory of myth overlaid on myth an alien intentionality. Now I can add by way of clarification that the theory failed to respect the limits of the story. Note carefully what is being claimed in my indictment: it is not that the story *announces* limits but rather that the story as story *is* limit. There is no legitimate transgressing of these limits, whether in the interest of establishing the transcendent reality of the deities named in the stories or for the purpose of reconstructing some presupposed past of which the myths are thought to be a record. If these are illegitimate pursuits, what—it may be asked—are legitimate claims for the intentionality of myths that respect their narrative limits?

I suggest, along strict relational lines, that myths image reality as relatedness. I maintain, further, that the most economical reading of the stories, and hence the one most commensurate with their intentionality, notices one thing: characters in relation. The characters cannot be lifted out of the relationships, for in a fundamental sense they *are* the relationships. The primary disclosures given in the reading are neither clues to the existence of these characters in relation (the *dramatis personae*) "outside the story" as it were, nor guides to the reconstruction of what actually happened in the past life, that is, in the supposed real time of the characters. All such expectations derive from the referential paradigm. The religious stories commend themselves, rather, for their aesthetic and paradigmatic imaging of reality as relatedness. In light of what was claimed earlier about ontology and experience, it is appropriate to extend the statements about the intentionality of myth a step further: myths are archetypal images of what is fundamental, namely, *pure experience, immediacy, relating*. The myths archetypically image the same insight into reality that emerges in relational ontology. Nevertheless myths are not ontologies. The terms 'archetypal' and 'image(ing)' express the difference. It is the second of these terms I should like to develop first. Clarification of the first will appear later.

Imaging is what myths do. That they do it successfully is

largely an aesthetic affair. One could say that the imaging they
do is aesthetic disclosure.

I am not suggesting that this latter term 'disclosure' entails
the ancient doctrine which interprets the phrase "of the gods" as a
subjective genitive. Disclosure is used here in one sense only: in
myth what is present is re-*present*-ed. Following Gadamer, I interpret myth as the re-*present*-ation of what is at hand.[3] The
proper synonym for myth is thus symbol. One way of amplifying
the meaning of symbol is to differentiate it from a sign, the latter
being an arbitrary convention that points away from itself to
what is not present. A sign thus sign-als the reality of what is absent. Its inadequacy lies in the distance between its presence and
the absent thing signified. It seeks to authenticate the reality of
what is not at hand. Hence the great reticence of archetypal religious persons to provide signs, as for example when Jesus in the
synoptic accounts announces, "No sign will be given you except
the sign of Jonah" (Matt. 12:39; 16:4; Luke 11:29). I would resolve the apparent contradiction in this saying ("no sign except")
by arguing that the first occurrence of the phrase 'no sign' carries
the meaning assigned to the term in my previous discussion, while
the meaning of the final phrase is best captured in the translation
"instead I give you the symbol of Jonah." Mark's simpler form,
"no sign will be given this generation" (8:12), becomes commensurate with Matthew's and Luke's versions with the suggested interpretation of the latter. It also follows that the proper rendering
of the key word *sēmeion* in the Fourth Gospel is symbol rather
than sign.

In contrast to signs, symbols re-present the power of what is
present to announce itself. Put more forcefully, *presence* is the
announcement of reality as relatedness. Thus for relational hermeneutics the intentionality of myth is in full accord with the relational ontology outlined above.

I shall now indicate some of the implications of this relational understanding of myth and, in the process of doing so, shall
take the occasion to amplify some key notions only hinted at so
far. Attention will be confined to two implications that seem to
be the most far-reaching for the interpretation of religious texts

and of statements of belief modeled on them, namely, 1) the negation of the view that originative religious texts are historical
records and 2) a reinterpretation of the transcendent dimension
in the stories that defines them as religious.

The rise and fall of the faith-history paradigm

The real shibboleth of recent generations of Scripture scholarship in the West is neither the terms 'kerygma' nor 'hermeneutics', as is commonly supposed, but the term 'history' and its cog-
nates 'historical' and 'historicity'. Those conversant with the ebb
and flow of the various modern schools of interpretation of Scripture that have successfully commanded the loyalties of Jewish
and Christian scholars will realize how pervasive the term 'history' has been in defining their principal differences. As one long
caught up in this phenomenon, I now wonder why it exercised
control over my mind for so long. And, further, why do modern
sacred phrases like 'God acting in history' and 'the historical Jesus'
seem to lose their cogency, and hence their urgency, once a relational theory of religious texts is espoused?

The claim that a deep commitment to historicism permeates
modern Western scriptural interpretation needs no documentation. The unexamined assumption of that historicism is that *narrative* implies *record*. Anyone conversant with the complex character of modern biblical criticism over the past two centuries is
aware of the extensive investment of energy directed toward the
reconstruction of "what really happened" behind the documents,
whether it be the lives of the Patriarchs, the deeds of Moses, or the
life of Jesus. I am well aware that in recent scholarship objections
have been raised about these efforts at reconstruction on the
grounds that faith is not well served by such activities. I should
like to suggest a more text-related objection, namely, that these
well-intentioned exercises in historical reconstruction do not respect the *limits* of the stories as stories. To treat such narratives as
records, whether judged historically valuable or worthless, results in a shift away from the stories to what is not present, that is,
to some previous time in which the actions are thought to be located. In such treatment the text ceases to function as *image* or

symbol and becomes an *organon* for solving questions foreign to originative religious texts. The result is that the text—as we used to say—becomes a pretext.

My remarks are not to be construed as a negative judgment on the work done legitimately by historians. Such interests seem essential to the self-consciousness of a civilized culture. What we learn from historians of genius, moreover, is that texts are also historical phenomena, often of significance equal to, or greater than, the events supposedly reported in texts under consideration by the historian. It must also be noted that certain newer methodologies in Scripture scholarship—as redaction criticism, literary criticism, structuralism, genre criticism, and such—seem to be more aware of the need to respect the narrative-text as *limit*, that is, as something in itself.

The legitimate extension of the principles of this relational hermeneutic to all texts of "eminent literature" should be apparent, especially to those who have pondered the deeply perceptive hermeneutical insights of Gadamer, expressed programmatically in his work *Truth and Method*. That I came to so similar an understanding of hermeneutics out of a quite different matrix reinforces my confidence in the viability of this relational theory of interpretation. Whether the relational ontology from which it is derived would be attractive to him I cannot say. I should now like to develop the theme of the religious dimension of myth.

The religious-transcendent dimension of myth

Lest it seem that relational hermeneutics is insensitive to the religious dimensions of myths, I shall attempt to explicate in relational terms what the expression 'of the gods' means within mythic consciousness. What follows is intended to apply with equal validity to originative religious stories and to statements of belief modeled on them.

The first step toward this explication is the simple translation of the phrase 'stories of the gods' into the generic formulation *God-Language*. Some might prefer the term 'God-Talk', suggested by Macquarrie, but they must bear in mind that he coined it as a characterization of theology. God-Language seems to me best suited to represent the distinctive dimension of mythical discourse.

God-Language, suggested by the primordial symbols of mythical stories, functions, as does every symbol, both as *disclosure* and as *limit*. As was claimed earlier, myths disclose through imaging. The question as to what is disclosed has partially been answered by the attendant claim that myths image reality as relatedness. To the extent that this claim is interpreted exhaustively as *the* nature of experience, no transexperiential conclusions being admitted, this interpretation of God-Language appears formally similar to Bultmann's theory that the task of the interpreter is to explicate the understanding of existence the myth is trying to express.[4] The existentialist anthropology Bultmann developed as the exhaustive disclosure of myth functioned well for a generation suspicious of ontology. A rationalistic corollary of this existentialist reduction was the call to eliminate the cosmology in which the story was set. A relational reassessment of myth does not proceed by eliminating anything; rather, it treats the myth as an inviolate whole. As I see it in retrospect, Bultmann made two questionable assumptions fatal to his program, the first being that *pre*scientific means *un*scientific, hence untrue, from which it follows that the cosmological elements must be stripped away if one is to understand myth. This dubious assumption originated within his rationalistic bias against primitive modes of expression. The second assumption was that myth "speaks of the other world in terms of this world, and of the gods in terms derived from human life."[5] The relational hermeneutics advanced here argues the inverse, namely, that in myth this world is presented in terms of the other world, that is to say, experience in terms of God-Language. The net effect of this inversion is to focus the interpretation of myth on experience; the transexperiential is excluded *per definitionem*. That this move entails no reduction of the essential function of God-Language—whether as present in originative religious stories or in statements of belief modeled thereon—remains to be shown.

The explication of the character and function of God-Language forces us back to the ontological priority of relation. While it has been maintained in this essay that objects and object-selves are—like subjects—derivative notions, I have carefully re-frained from referring to these objects as forms of experiential otherness. For it is central to the relational paradigm that in pure activity the experiential self and experiential other are not yet dif-ferentiated. Unlike coaspectual derivatives, their reality is coac-tuality, mutuality. A vestige of this relational affirmation lingers in the coaspectuality of the subject-object derivatives. Only the notion of mutuality functions ontologically in the delineation of the complex character of otherness which follows:

1) when the experiencing entails *restricted* mutuality, the experiential other yields upon reflection the notion of phenome-nal things;

2) when the experiencing entails *full* mutuality, the exper-ential other yields upon reflection the notion of object-selves.

Myth represents the fundamentality of mutuality dramati-cally and eminently through a characterization distinguished by the primary role of the Eminent Other. Failure to understand the narrative character of myth has led to the interpretation of the Eminent One as "the Wholly Other," a notion which appears er-roneous in view of the intrinsic mutuality of otherness. The fact that myth has been so interpreted is best explained by the *allzu-menschlich* human proclivity for ontologizing derivative notions, a state of affairs bemoaned by Whitehead in his classic phrase "the fallacy of misplaced concreteness." Only through a referential reading of God-Language does myth express Absolute Otherness. Relationally interpreted, God-Language is the announcement of the Eminent Other. Does such a claim entail the legitimacy of in-terpreting the Eminent Other as person? It would seem that the ascribing of personhood to God is tantamount to the ascribing of independent subjectivity to object-selves, raised to the eminent degree. There is some support for this suggestion from a state-ment in Whitehead's *Process and Reality*:[6]

> Creativity is here termed 'God', because the contemplation of our natures, as enjoying real feelings derived from the timeless sources of all order, acquires that 'subjective form' of refreshment and companionship at which religions aim.

The unique feature of God-Language, usually expressed by

the term 'transcendence', I have called *eminence*. Eminence
means that God-Language represents a derivative imaging of
experience-considered-as-a-Totality, coaspectual with "world-
language," or cosmology. Such is the basis of my view that theology and cosmology are complementary, that neither is absolute.[7]

The eminence of the other lies, not in some presumed "primordial nature" of the Other, but in the eminence of certain relations, expressed in words like worshiping, reverencing, trusting,
believing. An example may add a dimension of clarity to the
highly idiosyncratic language I am using. Take two sentences,
grammatically similar:

    A. I trust (a) person.

    B. I trust (in) God.

In sentence A, relationally understood, the "I" and the "person"
are regarded as derivatives of the fundamental activity, "trusting." It is the dimension of full mutuality inherent in the verbal
notion of "trusting" that yields the coderivative, "the personal
other." That same mutuality inheres by analogy in the verb "trusting" in Sentence B, though every user would admit that it is raised
to the eminent degree. Since no ontological principle deriving
from the relational ontology presented in this essay warrants the
category of "eminent mutuality," it is apparent that in Sentence
B, we have to do, not with God-as-*the*-Other, but with the Eminent Other, that is, with God-Language. We are, in sum, dealing
with myth, whether in the form of "eminent literature" or of belief statements utilizing its prime categories. This conclusion sup-
ports the definition of myth throughout this paper as *stories* of the
gods. In myth, interpreted rigorously in terms of a relational paradigm, one has to do, not with God existing *beyond* (i.e., trans-)
experience, but rather with the other of eminent imaging, that
is, with a coaspectual imaging of experience-considered-as-a-
Totality.

The reference to religious acts invites amplification. Such
acts are not categorically distinguished by the usual criteria of 1)
greater intensity, 2) ritual or moral purity, or 3) the eminence of
the object. Rather, they merit the qualifier "religious" because
they (re)-en-act the myth. Through religious acts the religious
person dwells within the mythical matrix of meaning. No one

worships save within the matrix of myth; thus worshiping is an entering into mythic drama in the role defined for devotees in the myth. For this reason myth and ritual belong to the very essence of religion.

NOTES

1. Martin Heidegger, *Being and Time*, tr. John Macquarrie and Edward Robinson (New York: Harper & Brothers, 1962 [1st German ed., 1927]), p. 19.

2. G. E. Moore, *Philosophical Studies* (1922; reprint ed., Totowa, NJ: Littlefield, Adams, 1968), p. 288.

3. Hans-Georg Gadamer, *Truth and Method* (New York: The Seabury Press, 1975 [1st German ed., 1960; 2nd., 1965]), p. 136. Gadamer's wording is "a symbol manifests as present something that really is present."

4. Rudolf Bultmann, "The New Testament and Mythology," in *Kerygma and Myth I*, ed. Hans Werner Bartsch (London: S.P.C.K., 1953 [orig. German ed., 1941]), p. 16.

5. Ibid., p. 10.

6. Alfred North Whitehead, *Process and Reality: An Essay in Cosmology* (1929; reprint ed., New York: Harper Torchbook, 1960), p. 47.

7. Harold H. Oliver, "The Complementarity of Theology and Cosmology," *Zygon: Journal of Religion and Science* 13 (March 1978): 19–33.

6

Religious and Poetical Speaking

HANS-GEORG GADAMER

FOR MANY YEARS I HAVE been concerned with the problems of poetical language and how such language works in the establishment of autonomous texts. By autonomous texts I mean texts which interpret themselves insofar as one needs no additional information about the occasion and the historical circumstances of their composition. Here I will try to contribute to the ongoing discussion concerning the inadequacy of referential interpretations of religious speaking, or "God-Language," by offering a hermeneutical description of the relationship between poetical and religious texts.

Whoever tries to give account of the achievements of the Western cultural traditions is confronted with the fact that in other regions of this planet we find very different and high cultural traditions which cannot be subordinated to or integrated into a Western conceptual framework. In our case it is important to recognize that outside of the Western tradition one cannot differentiate philosophical, religious, and poetical speaking. It is pointless and meaningless to ask, for example, whether the sayings of Lao-tse are the work of a philosopher, a religious man, or a poet. But "Is Dante a poet or a theologian?" and "Is Plato a philosopher or a poet?" do not seem to be idle questions to us because we have developed specific classifications concerning religious, philosophical, and poetical discourse and literature. We Westerners are challenged to apply such distinctions to other traditions adequately but also to avoid superficiality in understanding them strictly by the headlines of our own historical tradition.

Hermeneutics is the basis for the whole complex of the humanities. Hermeneutics means "theory of interpretation." In a more radical sense, however, interpretation is not just a specialty of the humanities and of our encounter with texts. Because the world is organized by linguistically articulated social patterns, interpretation is the primary access to our experience of the world. Learning a vernacular language means being introduced into the experience of the world. Even our epistemological approach to knowledge and cognition cannot avoid passing through this hermeneutical dimension, that is, the ongoing reinterpretation of statements which are themselves interpretations of our being-in-a-world. Therefore hermeneutics is for everyone.

The model which underlies this general hermeneutical approach is the model of question and answer. Indeed, I am convinced that no possible statement can really be understood if it is not understood as an answer to a possible question. To find and elaborate the question, that is the question! For it is the question which gives us access to an adequate interpretation of a statement as a possible answer to the question. I found some confirmation for the general hermeneutical validity of this model of question and answer in Collingwood's well-known autobiography in which he refers to the logic of question and answer in describing his own investigation of Britain's prehistory. Collingwood's logic is presented there in a little too simplified form, but at least he explains well the basic hermeneutical relevance of the logical correspondence of question and answer. My thesis is that the problem of hermeneutical access to experience, that is, the epistemological relevance of the linguistic layer of our world experience, is closely connected with this structure of question and answer. In the basic form of a dialogue we find the process by which a common language between two speakers comes to be.

The logical structure of dialogue must be the guideline for any research in hermeneutics. In my own hermeneutical theory, at least, I try to demonstrate that it is this living actuality of language and not language in its abstraction which elucidates most clearly what happens in speech.[1] However, religious and poetical speaking in the West are not squarely placed in this basic hermeneutical dimension of question and answer. On the contrary, we encounter poetical and religious speaking which occur independently of the dialogical process of language. We must deal with autonomous texts, which in a sense are independent from the ongoing flux of reason and discourse which constitute the life of a speaking community. Such texts are detached from their originating situations.

In pointing to the fact that there are well-distinguished autonomous texts which address us, we are confronted with the special Western way of thinking, with stark, conceptual thinking and the analytical "splitting power" implicit in it. The splitting off of poetical, religious, and philosophical discourse in the West so that speech is no longer the monolithic unity that it is in Chinese or in Indian traditions is first established by the Greco-Christian tradition. Because of this dividing or splitting of the three forms of thinking and speaking, philosophy of religion has the special problem of ascertaining the interrelationship of these different forms. I am here concerned especially with the affiliation and the discrimination of two of these forms: poetical and religious discourse.

In a way poetical and religious speaking are inseparable. Because they are nonreferential, religious and poetical speaking transcend the requirements of formal conceptualization and are, in a way, self-fulfilling languages. As we know from Kant's famous description of aesthetic judgments, when one experiences the beautiful in nature and in works of art, one cannot exhaust the meaning of these experiences by concepts.

The interrelationship of these different forms of speaking might be stated as it appears in the dissociation of poetical and philosophical speaking in the movement of the Greek enlightenment. We might first study the relationship of both forms of speaking in the philosophical work of Plato. Plato unquestionably mixes the poetic and conceptual forms of language, and he is well aware of the tension between them. He speaks of the old struggle between poets and philosophers in the development of Greek culture. The so-called theologians of Greek antiquity were, in fact, their poets. Homer and Hesiod, who were the first whose poetical texts were preserved in written form, are called theologians by Aristotle. But then the early Greek thinkers raised their audacious heads and asked such tricky questions as "What was first?" "What was in the beginning?" "How could it begin?" "What will be in the end?" and so on. All these questions were formulated or communicated by poetry in imitation of Homer's hexameter or by a monumental prose. They used Homeric style or at least Homeric vocabulary for such un-Homeric matters and problems as "Is there something?" "Is there nothing?" "What is being?" It is a good illustration of the old struggle between poets and philosophers—and every struggle presupposes a common ground—that the language of the philosophical poets itself is a mixture of epic words and forms and philosophical concepts. The power of the Homeric tradition was strong enough to overcome even such a logical genius as Parmenides. The same problem occurs even in the writings of Plato, so that it is an open question whether or not and to what degree Plato uses religious discourse—in the authentic sense of the word—in composing his myths. Obviously the marvelous mixing of philosophical and poetical speaking is one of the striking features of Plato's dialogical work and provides its authentic religious color.

The second dissociation which brings our problem into perspective is the dissociation of worship and faith. This also seems to me a special experience of Western civilization. We no longer have, at least since Luther and the Reformation generally, unambiguous evidence of a unity of worship and religious behavior. We are faced with the precarious and intricate question as to how far we can fulfill and sustain the whole work of cult, prayer, and benediction, since the sincerity of faith is at stake. This dissociation, of course, has been happening in Christianity since its inception, and it is basic to the entire formulation of my problem. Without this transition of Christianity into a religion of the Holy Book and the right dogmatic, the confrontation of poetical and religious texts would not have the significance that it has for us. It is the claim of scripture not to be *poesie* but to be truth. The problem which here arises as the common point between poetry and Christian tradition is that both have primary identity as texts. Two words which are quite common for us all fix this point: literature and scripture.

Both words are deeply connected with the art of writing and the written forms of texts and are used to indicate the special excellence of some forms of writing. It is clear that for written texts in general hermeneutics gains a primary function, not only for such excellent texts as scripture and literature. The general concern of hermeneutics is to make understandable what is difficult to understand, and one special case of it is to reawaken frozen letters to speech, in other words, "to let speak again" what is fixed by signs and letters. In this sense one can define the whole task of hermeneutics in this way: to let speak again what was spoken and what is fixed as spoken in the frozen form of written or printed words and letters. But it is an even more striking task to let speak again what is fixed in the form of autonomous texts which are completely separated from the occasions of ordinary communication, texts which have no special address and are not embedded in special occasions. We call them literary texts. In this case the problem of interpretation and understanding is most difficult. Again the same task remains—"to let it speak again"—and that means to constitute a new immediate exchange between the given text and the new reader and interpreter. Religious and poetical texts are in this eminent sense "autonomous texts." They are without a special address, but they address us all the same.

But there is nevertheless a basic difference between religious and poetical texts, between scripture and literature, and that is the difference in their form of anonymous address. It is not immediately apparent that literature and scripture have such a different form of address, but I think this is the case, and it is certainly the case as far as the New Testament is concerned. Literature, I suggest, has an indeterminate address. It is not written just for the critics in contemporary periodicals, nor is it normally written just for posterity, although this may be the deeper hope of the author. It is, in general, written in an anonymous form for people of today and of tomorrow, and many people of tomorrow are from yesterday!

How can literature hope to achieve this goal? Here we must enter into a study of the means by which language can stabilize itself in such a way that it becomes an autonomous text. An autonomous text is something which stands by itself, something to which one returns, a text which one may read again and again and which gains more and more richness when it becomes familiar. It is a text which one may even have learned by heart. This is quite different from ordinary language which we readily leave behind us. In ordinary speech our interest is that of discerning that to which the language points and which we expect and anticipate, as well as the momentary reaction of the other to whom we are speaking. But eminent, "literary" texts are dazzling concentrations of their own presence and evocative power. Thus, even occasional aspects of such a text—all of its historical *kairoi*—are quite incidental to an appreciative reading of a text. In the "Songs of Pindar," for example, the occasion is itself presented through the praise of victors in racing competitions. Certainly we learn something from the ancient commentaries about the dynasty of the victor and the special conditions of this racing. But to enjoy Pindar we do not need this special occasional information. How is it possible that lacking such information, we can read the "Songs of Pindar" without any loss of enjoyment? How is it possible for the occasional product of a poet to be more than an occasional product and to become a work, a piece of classic literature?

This special question of what I called the autonomy of a literary text cannot be pursued here, however. Here we will focus on scripture and its quite different literary character.

Scripture and the message which is conveyed by scripture do not have an anonymous address in the same sense as literature has. Scripture claims to be addressed only to the community of believers. That is certainly an essential character of the Holy Scripture. But in the same moment the address of Scripture is, in the words of Luther, *pro me*, "for me, for myself." We have to clarify the double-sidedness by which the Word, which is said by God, is speaking to me. To describe this special character of the address and presence of the text of the Bible I would like to refer to what one calls a *promise*. A promise is something which is not just a statement, not a judgment, not a pronouncement which stands by itself. I cannot make a promise by my own without acceptance on the part of the one who receives it. For example, if I were an alcoholic and I said to my wife, "Oh, that is the last bottle I will drink in my life," and if she knows me well, she would say, "It's better not to promise." That example is perhaps a little mundane, but it illustrates what the Holy Scripture is about.

Scripture, and here I am referring especially to the New Testament, is an offer, and it depends on the reader, on the listener, on the community as to how far they will accept it. The nature of message, in the religious sense of the Bible, depends absolutely on response from the believer who *accepts* the assuring or promising message.

But of course that is a very particular example of religious speech and peculiar to the Christian belief in the message of the Gospel. It is not quite the same in other "religions of the book," like Islam, and it is quite different in religions which know no holy books at all or in which holy books have a subordinated function. Therefore, we must extend our question beyond that of the Gospel to the broader field of religious speaking and language.

The technical term for the form in which religious texts speak is myth. The word *mythologein*, indeed, has to do with the act of speaking. Myth means a tale to be conveyed and to be verified by nothing else than the act of telling it. A myth which can be proved or verified by something outside of the living oral or written religious tradition is not really myth. Thus the only good definition of myth is that *myth neither requires nor includes any possible verification outside of itself.* Of course stories about God and man, of the dying and resurrected Jesus as the Christ, and many other stories in different religious and cultural traditions have a verifiable content. But what claims to be the truth is not the story, but what it means for the fate of man, his expectations and his hope. From a hermeneutical point of view we must abstract from this dogmatic content and concentrate on *narration* as one of the characteristic features of religious speaking.

In narration something is reported as that which happened "once upon a time." We can study the special character of narration and uncover some of the unique structures of narration that are, for example, most clearly evident in fairy tales. In the narration of fairy tales there is a floating richness of possible variation, of possible continuation. The famous fairy tales of the Brothers Grimm always include the formula endings "and if they didn't die, they live even today." While that ending is always a disappointment, it also lets us feel the infinite richness of events as the subjects of additional possible narration. It is a special feature of narration that one can never exhaust what one can tell. Insofar as narration is characteristic of a religious tradition and proclamation, the tradition remains open to a whole dimension of possible stories with new and different content. This special openness cannot be conceptualized and formally grasped in the abstract, structural analysis of statements and their dogmatic meanings.

Narration, then, is a kind of representation (*Vorstellung*). Because of all the subjectivistic connotations one has in mind when one uses the word 'representation' to translate *Vorstellung*, it is important to remember that the meaning of representation which is closest to *Vorstellung* is akin to the use of the word in geometry where one "makes something visible" through the use of an illustrating figure. *Vorstellung* is not something subjective; it is not a sort of substitute for something else. In the figure the thing is re-presented so that it is present. For example, the flag of a nation is a representation of the nation, a substitute for the presence of its authority, and is not merely a sign by which we are referring to something else. The flag, so to speak, is the *presence* of the nation, so that an attack against the flag is not just the destroying of a sign but an act of political blasphemy or, in battle, of dishonor.

It is the special feature of narrative structure that it can never be exhaustive or definite, and this means, of course, that it is always open to the poetic imagination. This is especially clear in Greek history where religion is not based on books. Of course, there were special sects and religious movements where the function of the sacred book, the *hieros logos*, poses difficult questions. But we can abstract from such particular cases and point out the fact that the official Greek religion was tremendously liberal and tolerant in repeating and interpreting again and again the whole mythic tradition. It was almost a point of honor for a poet to find a new, sophisticated version of an old mythic story. We can see this, for example, in the different dramatic representations of the story of Iphigenia. We know the Greek tragedians risked new and audacious interpretations of the story. In contrast to them, at least to someone as inventive as Euripedes, Goethe appears to be a tame and faithful believer in what he found in the Greek religious tradition. Anything seems to be allowed for the Greek poets and philosophers, not to mention the comedians. No facts, no doctrines were taboo. The liberty which characterizes their religious attitude extends even to the proper names of the gods themselves. The Greeks did not feel certain about the gods' authentic names. Even in worshipping Zeus they were never sure whether or not he should be addressed by this name; it was just the way it was done.

In this lack of definiteness religious experience and language are strikingly similar to music. In music we find a similar hovering feeling of vagueness and significance. We know that music is not at all arbitrary or unarticulated, since it obeys strong and almost mathematical laws of symmetry, construction, repetition, response, and so on. But at the same time music retains a certain floating wordlessness. It is like a lack of words, but it is not just a lack; it is more like a door that is waiting for the key word that will open its meaning. By its exceptional transition into song Beethoven's Ninth Symphony is a special illustration of this longing of music for linguistic achievement. Indeed, some nostalgia for words and word-language seems inherent in music. My main point in comparing religious language to music, however, is the liberty of interpretation they hold in common.

While musical reproduction involves freedom of interpretation, nevertheless such interpretation is not arbitrary. There is no lack of canons of adequacy. For example, I once heard Furtwängler, the famous German conductor, direct a performance of Bach. The music was played with tremendous dynamics and in romantic style. It was marvelously done, but it was no longer the well-calculated contrapuntal universe of Bach. It was Furtwängler's interpretation indeed, but in this case one could say that it was not quite adequate. Although the performance was well done, one felt there was something wrong, a disjointedness between the perfect interpretation and the work itself. This example raises the question of what "meaning" means in music. There are indeed difficult problems as to how music can be loaded with meanings without words. Yet we know that there must be something of meaning there. Every day we discriminate between light and heavy, serious and gay music, even when the composers are cautious enough to restrain their advice to mere indications of tempo. Even the tempo indications have an intrinsic meaning for the composition, so that violating them deforms the work.

There is something similar happening with myths and their floating series of interpretations. It is especially the function of proper names to stimulate the interpreter-poet; they play a decisive role within the mythical imagination and creativity. In spite of the liberality of their use, names are perhaps the most constant thing in mythical tradition, far more persistent and stable than the formal interrelationships of the mythical algebra which is elucidated marvelously by Lévi-Strauss. Considering how proper names invite the religious-poetical imagination, we have some guideline for the question as to how much religious speaking fluctuates between liberty and authenticity.

This general character of mythical tradition stands in striking contrast to that of Christianity. The Christian religion is closely related to the holy book of Judaism and introduces itself as the fulfillment of the messianic expectations of Israel. It also shares the special claim of Judaism to have the one, unique God who is the protector of the elected people. Its own story, the Gospel, the *evangelium* of salvation and the character of promise which is included in the story of Jesus, shares the special privilege of the Judaic tradition over against the pagans. With its promise of salvation and its concern with mission to the world, Christianity even goes beyond Judaism. It is in demanding nothing else than belief, however, that the Christian tradition is distinguished from other mythical traditions as well as from any form of literature. Even to be an author means something special for the New Testament. Franz Overbeck, the church historian and friend of Nietzsche, called the Gospel not literature but *Urliteratur*. He meant by it, and I think he is correct, that the authors of the New Testament are not so much authors in the usual sense of the word but rather they are witnesses or the witnesses of witnesses. We know, of course, that every witness has his special view and pre-understanding. Modern theology has learned to discriminate these authors and to discern their view as dogmatic intentions by analyzing, comparing, and combining all our knowledge of the tradition they represent. In any case the authors are not just conveyors of a floating mythical tradition; they trace themselves back to witnesses who should be believed. Of course, to accept the message remains an act of personal decision in which both the belief in the reliability of the witnesses and the acceptance of the promise are joined. That is precisely the reason why historical criticism can never destroy the religious authority of this book.

Realizing the special character of the New Testament, we understand that *hermeneutics has a special and eminent function where the tradition of Christian faith is concerned.* This function is no longer that of hermeneutics in the general sense where, for the interpretation of literary texts (whether religious, poetic, or legal), we must apply some common rules of interpretation and some special knowledge. Certainly there are points that biblical and general hermeneutics hold in common. The reader of the Bible must know language, grammar, syntax, the historical conditions, and all the circumstances which are relevant for a given text. In this sense interpreting a biblical text is no special and exceptional hermeneutical situation. Indeed, here it is inappropriate to claim inspiration, which, as a matter of fact, would prevent any rational understanding of the text.

Nevertheless the general rules of hermeneutics and general scholarship do not represent the cardinal hermeneutical problem for the understanding of the New Testament. Although here there is more than the usual alienation and difficulty which occur in any form of fixed texts, one can overcome these problems by scholarship and hermeneutical skills. In the case of the New Testament, however, something especially incomprehensible provokes and challenges human self-understanding. It is the challenge that merit is secondary and faith is all. To put it another way: for the member of the Jewish community for whom the Old Testament is the holy book, the Law and obedience to the Law and to the will of God is the absolute demand and the primary interest of exegesis. That is quite easy to understand. But the novel message of the New Testament that faith is a gift of grace seems to be incomprehensible.

It may be comprehensible enough that merits alone are not sufficient to guarantee restitution in immortality and the benefits of the Holy God. But that salvation depends solely on this act of faith and belief and on nothing else appears really scandalous, and that is precisely the message of the New Testament. Certainly the notion that only the breakdown of our human self-understanding and our unconditional surrender to the savior—and nothing else—can help us to overcome death and the anxiety concerning death which is rooted in the human soul is highly scandalous and quite unique.

Here hermeneutics acquires a profound religious character since it no longer has to do with a method or with the skill of our rational faculty. New Testament hermeneutics has the special task of making acceptable what seems to be fundamentally incomprehensible: that faith is not the product of a believer's merit but an act of grace. Hermeneutics in this field is not just scholarly work, although it includes scholarly work. That is the reason why the theologian must be a scholar. But as a preacher he is more. The sermon, especially in the Protestant tradition, is an essential part of the service. The pastor in interpreting the message functions as a witness for the work of the Holy Spirit. In the same way all his scholarship and his skill serves this end. Every other form of religious speaking which occurs in the Christian cult seems to me ultimately related to this essential appeal to faith, and therefore it is always the rhetoric of faith which corresponds to God-Language.

One could ask Is poetical experience not also a provocation and a challenge which shocks us? For example, the recognition we have of ourselves through encountering the tragedy of King Oedipus is radically disorienting. Are we really as blind as the blinded hero? In such a manner the work of art may have the power to destroy our illusions and our self-assurance. Although almost every work of art can be experienced as a kind of provocation, such provocations are not the same work of challenge we confront in the New Testament. To understand the absolute and radical incomprehensibility of the Christian message something other is at stake than the dimensions of our self-understanding. There is a parallel to the sort of self-understanding that emerges in the confrontation with a work of art:

Da ist keine Stelle, die Dich nicht sieht.
Du musst dein Leben ändern.[2]

But conversion is something else, at least in the Christian

view. Perhaps in every form of religious experience it goes beyond our self-understanding. The naïve form of negotiations with the gods which occur in the pagan service is perhaps a degeneration of the authentic religious experience. However, in the case of the Christian message we have the exceptional and extreme situation in which no basis whatsoever for any form of rights over against the divine is preserved.

NOTES

1. In structural linguistics, by contrast, we have the abstract thematization of the structure of language. I have no objection to such study in itself, but an approach which abstracts from any content that is conveyed by language and suggests that this abstract structure is the main point in language seems to be narrow and prejudicial.

2. "For there is no place that does not see you,
   you must change your life."

The word 'place' here refers to the world of the work of art. From "The Archaic Torso of Apollo," *The Poetry of Rainer Maria Rilke*, tr. M. D. Herter Norton (New York: Norton, 1938), p. 181. *Ed.*

7
Myth, Symbol, and Metaphorical Truth

ALAN M. OLSON

FEW SCHOLARS IN OUR TIME have dealt as creatively and comprehensively with the subjects of myth, symbol, and metaphor as Paul Ricoeur. Indeed, there can be no discussion of these subjects today without reference to the work of Ricoeur since his investigations cut across disciplinary lines in a way that provokes attention from many different angles. In what follows I will discuss certain aspects of Ricoeur's analysis of metaphorical discourse in relation to the question What is the *truth* of myth, symbol, and metaphor? I begin by describing Ricoeur's *tensive theory of metaphorical truth* and compare it with Cassirer's understanding of the *radical metaphor*, noting that while their strategies of analysis are similar, their conclusions are quite different. For Cassirer the tensive character of metaphor has reference only to epistemology and the symbolic constitution of reality, but for Ricoeur this tensive quality is also related to what he terms the 'textures' of reality. After this I discuss Ricoeur's treatment of what Roman Jakobson has termed *metaphoric split reference* in relation to Karl Jaspers' philosophy of *boundary* or *limit situations* (*Grenzsituationen*) in order to locate more precisely what I consider to be the anthropological and existential foundations of metaphorical predication and discourse. Finally, I provide some reflections on what Ricoeur terms the *spheres of discourse* known as the poetical and the philosophical with a view to Heidegger and the fundamental problem of ontology. Here the critical question has to do with *mediation* and its role in ascertaining the truth of myth, symbol, and metaphor.

99

RICOEUR'S TENSIVE THEORY
OF METAPHORICAL TRUTH

Prior to dealing with what Ricoeur considers to be the nature of metaphorical truth it is necessary to recall a bit of the overall structure of the remarkable work within which it is developed. *The Rule of Metaphor*[1] consists of eight separate studies of metaphor, and each may be viewed, Ricoeur suggests, as complete in itself. However, there is also a larger question that guides the work as a whole, namely, "*What* philosophy is *implied* in the movement that carries the investigation [of metaphor] from rhetoric to semantics and from sense to reference?" (RM, 257). It is this question that concerns us and it is raised both inductively and hermeneutically.

On the inductive side Ricoeur seems to be suggesting that at some point during an empirical and linguistic analysis of metaphor the larger philosophical question will emerge as a matter of course and even necessity. Thus as investigation moves from the analysis of metaphor as an isolatable unit of language or word (rhetoric and semiology), to the consideration of the nature and meaning of the metaphorical phrase or sentence (semantics), and finally to the meaning of the metaphorical work or text (hermeneutics), Ricoeur insists that such analyses and considerations are incomplete until one finally asks what metaphorical discourse has to contribute to our understanding of reality as such (metaphysics). On the hermeneutical side it is a strategy that is informed by the dynamics of Ricoeur's own version of the hermeneutical circle and the movement of investigation from whole to part and from part to whole. The movement from whole to part (what Ricoeur variously terms as the "descending analytic" or "archeological moment") is the normal work of criticism. To know something is to take it apart in scrutinizing its structures, its background, its style, genre, and so on. The implication, or more precisely the presupposition, of this model of analysis and criticism is that once one has "gotten to the bottom of things," so to speak, one will know what it means. But hermeneutic philosophy reminds us that this is not necessarily the case and that such an approach may, in fact, actually prevent us from discovering what the text means. Thus Ricoeur insists that the downward movement of analysis must be complemented by the upward movement of interpretation or saying what the text means. This movement from part to whole (variously termed by Ricoeur as an "ascending dialectic" or the "teleological moment") is the proper work of hermeneutics. But this movement from part to whole is not automatic. It is rather the result of a kind of wager that the text *has* a meaning, in other words, that it has semantic autonomy even before the work of analysis and interpretation takes place. Such wagers may be either covert or overt: covert in the case of an interpretation that assumes to transcend the subjectivity of the subject doing the interpretation, and overt when the element of the interpreter's subjectivity is both acknowledged and understood.

What this means is that one can never claim to have presented the definitive interpretation of a text. One rather moves between interpretations as one moves between the "obscurity" and the "ideality" limits of analysis and interpretation. This double movement, however, is not circular in the vicious sense. It is rather circular in the sense of what Jaspers calls the *Encompassing*, namely, as analysis and interpretation turn on the double foci of obscurity and ideality and continue this movement, interpretation and understanding become more encompassing and comprehensive without ever assuming that the end point of interpretation, so to speak, has ever been reached.

Ricoeur begins his study of metaphor with Aristotle and the observation that for Aristotle metaphor is located somewhere "between rhetoric and poetics." Metaphor is perceived by Aristotle on the side of rhetoric as a device for "persuasion in oral discourse" and on the side of poetics as a means for "the mimesis of human action in tragic poetry" (RM, 3). Of even greater significance for Ricoeur is Aristotle's refusal to view metaphor as merely an ornament of language that is devoid of ontological implication. Metaphors are rather *referential* in the sense that they provide the basis for a "rediscription of reality" and present things "in a state of activity" (RM, 307). Hence, metaphors are in some sense transparent to the nature of reality in a way that other forms of language are not.

With metaphor thereby located in Aristotle as a kind of

boundary linguistic phenomenon that is strangely appropriate to man's "being in the middle of things," it is not surprising that Ricoeur should find taxonomic and semiotic analyses of metaphor less than completely adequate. Indeed, it is not until metaphor is better understood as a "figure of deviation" within the structure of a complete phrase or sentence that its nature can be more fully comprehended. For this to happen one must move from a rhetorical and semiotic to a semantic analysis of the innovative character of metaphor. To put the matter another way, at the level of a word by word analysis of language the metaphorical word seems misplaced and inappropriate, a "deviant denomination." But at the level of the phrase or sentence the literal meaning of metaphor is displaced by means of what Ricoeur calls "impertinent predication," and the result is the creation of a new and different meaning. The question is "what does the metaphorical statement say about reality" (RM, 216) in contrast to statements that are nonmetaphorical?

To raise the question of *metaphorical truth* is to raise the problem of *reference*, in other words, To what reality does the metaphorical utterance refer or point to? Here Ricoeur accepts the classical formulation of Gottlob Frege concerning the sense (*Sinn*), or "what" a proposition states and "how" it is stated, and reference (*Bedeutung*), or "that about which" something is stated in terms of its meaning or denotation (RM, 217). Ricoeur does not accept, however, the positivist notion that metaphorical utterances are merely connotative and so trapped within the emotive structures of subjectivity that they cannot be verified. It is his stated intention, therefore, "to do away with the restriction of reference to scientific statements" and to "reformulate" a postulate of reference that can do justice to the unique case that metaphor represents in a work of poetry or fiction (RM, 221, 227). Ricoeur's reformulation reads as follows: "The literary work, through the structure proper to it, displays a world only under the conditions that the reference of descriptive discourse is suspended" (RM, 221). What he means by this is that the primary reference of the metaphorical utterance is *not* a first- or surface-level denotation but a "second-level denotation" in which the first level of meaning or reference is suspended. What is unique to metaphorical discourse, then, is *split reference* that comes about by way of an intentional equivocation, to use Aristotle's term, that makes it impossible to adjudicate its meaning by the standards of univocity that are proper only to scientifically descriptive statements about reality. "So it is," Ricoeur says summarily, "that just as the metaphorical statement captures its *sense* as metaphorical amidst the ruins of literal sense, it also captures its *reference* upon what might be called (in symmetrical fashion) its literal reference" (RM, 221).

Now this phenomenon of split reference for Ricoeur is more, obviously, than just a passing observation. "What is at stake," he says, "is nothing less than the meaning of the words *reality* and *truth* which [if Ricoeur is successful in clarifying the "virtual mode of reference" inherent in his tensive theory of metaphor] must themselves vacillate and become problematical" (RM, 229). What this demands is the location of the cause of the kind of foundering that occurs between one level of denotative reference and the semantic innovation that emerges through the disclosure of second-level denotative reference. The source of this tension for Ricoeur is to be found within the metaphoric copula itself. Just as the scientific model is deployed not for the sake of proof but as a means for "discovery through redescription" (RM, 240), so also the "living metaphor" is deployed not to prove that there is something "called metaphorical truth" (RM, 255) but as a means to "delexicalize" accepted meanings. When this happens we are reawakened to the polysemy of language, the instability of meaning, and the possibility of new meaning (RM, 246). Again, the power of metaphor to bring about this "semantic innovation" resides empirically in the metaphoric copula and its paradoxical "is/is-not" dialectic. Here then is the nodal point of split reference, for it is the metaphoric copula that brings about the intentional equivocation in which contraries are postulated seemingly in defiance of the law of contradiction. But this paradoxical predication is not to be viewed as an end in itself, for it is precisely by magnifying and exemplifying the tension inherent in the manner in which the bipolar, subject-object structure of experience is normally understood that metaphor is able somehow to transcend this apparent dichotomy. It is precisely in this sense, I think, that

as Paul Lehmann once put it, "metaphor catches the truth by per-
mitting it to be a lie." What is of decisive importance for Ricoeur,
however, is the maintenance of the *tension* inherent in the metaphoric copula; in other words, one must refrain from the tempta-
tion of absolutising either side of a split reference, for to do so
would be to reduce metaphor into something that it is not. Thus,
what we have termed the *boundary* character of metaphorical
discourse must, for Ricoeur, be preserved in order to see that "the
tension that affects the copula in its relational function also affects the copula in its existential function" and that is is precisely
this *tension* that "contains the key to the notion of metaphorical
truth" (RM, 248).

Now what is this *truth*? Thus far we have indicated that Ricoeur has located the source of split reference in the metaphoric
copula itself. But what he refers to as a tensive theory of metaphorical truth clearly implies more than merely the fact or truth
that there is something peculiar about the metaphoric copula.

Ricoeur attempts to clarify this question by contrasting what
he perceives to be two radically differing perspectives on the meaning of metaphor and, we might add, the meaning of myth and
symbol as well since the issues are the same. On the one hand there
is what Ricoeur typifies as the intuitionist or vitalist position that
claims, as in the case of Philip Wheelwright, where the meaning
of metaphor is understood through "presentational immediacy"
(RM, 251). On the other hand there is the manipulative-mythical
position that suggests, as in the case of Colin Turbayne and Gil-
bert Ryle, that metaphorical utterances are "intentional category
confusion" and the occasions for the fostering of superstitions and
bogus ontologies. While the former view has to its credit a profound sense of place of the creative imagination in metaphorical
utterances, it tends to drift into what Ricoeur terms a "primitive
animism" (RM, 255) and what John Findlay terms the "myth of
the immediate-immediate." The latter position has to its credit a
critical understanding of the manner in which metaphor *works*,
namely, that creative metaphorical utterances have the power to
clear away the husks of metaphors that have found their way into
lexicons. Such metaphors are dead in the sense that their meaning
is fixed. But it is a position that also presupposes a nominalistic
ontology that seemingly does not itself have to be justified (RM,

252). In short, what both positions lack is what Ricoeur terms "a tensional conception of truth."

Ricoeur's strategy of elucidating the evanescent character of metaphorical truth is not unlike that of Ernst Cassirer, but the outcome is quite different.[2] For Cassirer it is nineteenth-century romantic philosophers like Herder and Schelling who exemplify the vitalist-intuitionist position, who believe that the first and authentic language of man was "the sounding pantheon of nature" and that everything since can be counted as loss. On the other hand, the comparative philologists Adalbert Kuhn and Max Müller represent the positivistic-manipulative position and the notion that "mythology," in the celebrated phrase of Müller, "is but the disease of language." Like Ricoeur, Cassirer also refused to opt for either of these counterpositions as definitive, and he also insisted that theories of substitution and category transfer cannot fully account for what is going on in the metaphorical process. Like Ricoeur, Cassirer was also fascinated by the "spheres of discourse" known as the conceptual and poetical; how the mode of the former is that of logical and discursive "synthetic supplementation" through a process that abstracts from experience in order to isolate more and more effectively and precisely discrete particulars and their interrelatedness; how the mode of the latter is "compressive" unto the "single point" where, as in the notion of *pars pro toto*, "every part of the whole is the whole itself, and every specimen equivalent to the entire species" through "the leveling and extinction of specific differences."[3] One thinks, for example, of lines from William Blake's "Auguries of Innocence," namely, "To see the World in a Grain of Sand / And Heaven in a Wild Flower, / Hold Infinity in the palm of your hand / And Eternity in an hour." Cassirer, I think, would also agree with Ricoeur's contention out of Husserl that formal-conceptual discourse opens a yawning abyss between the similar and the same, the concrete and the universal, whereas poetical-metaphorical discourse tends to identify and even to obliterate these distinctions in the incarnate language of fleshly particularity and immediacy (RM, 301).

Yet there is an important difference. For Cassirer both kinds of discourse have their common origin in the transcendental imagination with the root or *radical metaphor* being understood as the point of their nascent origin. What this intersection reveals for Cassirer is, *not* the "schematic textures" of both the "interior life" and the "world" that so fascinate Ricoeur (RM, 255), but rather the manner in which there takes place the symbolic constitution by the transcendental imagination of what we call reality. What Ricoeur terms "the thinking-more of the imagination" that manifests itself so powerfully in the living metaphor points to a *beyond* or a *hidden-undisclosed-reality* that is closer to the concerns of Heidegger. In his aporetic reading of Kant, Heidegger maintains that "the act of pure intuition is essentially pure imagination" in that it "lets spring forth" that which is "present." "By this radical interrogation," Heidegger goes on to say, "Kant brought the possibility of metaphysics before the abyss. He saw the unknown: he had to draw back. Not only did the imagination fill him with alarm, but in the meantime between the first and second editions he had also come more and more under the influence of pure reason as such."[4] What is lost in the Kantian turn, according to Heidegger, is the original unity of pure apprehension, pure reproduction, and pure recognition in the "productive imagination" and its grounding in "primordial time." What is left are sensible intuitions and the transcendental categories of the "reproductive imagination."[5]

Ricoeur has trouble with the Heideggerian language of "primordiality" and "hiddeness" as we will see. For now suffice it to say that the "thinking more" of the creative-productive imagination is intrinsic to his notion of metaphorical truth in that it is what he calls the "vivifying principle" and the "soul" of interpretation (RM, 303). But the question still before us has to do with understanding the nature of metaphorical truth itself and not merely the processes by and through which it comes to be. To prepare for this task I will first explore what I perceive to be the connections between Ricoeur's theory of metaphorical truth and his philosophical anthropology.

METAPHORIC SPLIT REFERENCE
AND THE BOUNDARY SITUATION

"What we finally make out of metaphor," whether in theory or practice, as Elizabeth Sewell contends, "really depends on what we make out of the essential *morphe* of *anthropos*."[6] Because for her the "shape" of "man" is essentially metaphoric, metaphors are deployed as the ideal instruments of language "to build up the fusing of man and the universe."[7] As Ezra Pound exclaimed, "Man and earth are the two halves of the tally," for it is in man, as Goethe observed, "that nature and history coincide."

When Ricoeur asks, therefore, whether or not the tension that characterizes the metaphoric copula in its "relational function" does not also affect its "existential function" and that the answer to this question "contains the key to metaphorical truth" (RM, 248), I am suggesting that it is precisely this existential tension that is the origin of the tension in the relational function. Thus I will be arguing, first, that it is the tensive-boundary character of man's being in a world that is the precondition of metaphoric-symbolic utterances and, second, that it is because of this antecedent anthropological condition that metaphor both speaks and is transparent to the depths of human experience. Indeed, Ricoeur himself says that "the phenomenological objectivity of what commonly is called emotion or feeling is inseparable from the tensional structure of the truth of metaphorical statements that express the construction of the world by and with feeling. The possibility of textural reality is correlative to the possibility of a metaphorical truth of poetic schemata; the possibility of one is established at the same time as the other" (RM, 255).

Split reference, then, really mirrors a double dialectic, a dialectic that is operative both at the level of reference and also at the level of what Jaspers called *Existenz*. Now these are radical *boundary* images, and anyone who reads Ricoeur cannot fail to be impressed by his fondness for and sensitivity to the dialectical boundary language of the between. It is, of course, a language that has profound expressions in Plato's description of the Soul situated, so to speak, "between earth and heaven" (*metaxu kosmos kai ouranos*); in Descartes' characterization of man as "between" being and nonbeing; in Kant's epistemological formulations; and in the discourse of dialectical thinkers generally including Hegel, Heidegger, Tillich, and Gadamer. It is a language responsive to the limits and the boundaries of human experience and knowledge. It is the language that provides the basis for Ricoeur's elucidation of the drama of the divided man in his philosophy of will, whether it be his eidetic analysis of the voluntary and the involuntary, his empirics of fallibility and the pathetique of misery, or his mythics-symbolics of evil and the fault. In each case we see human nature as bounded and nonidentical with itself; in each case we are confronted by the phenomenology of split-reference, so to speak, or what Jaspers terms the phenomena of "disjunction." Thus, I am suggesting that the philosophy implied in Ricoeur's study of metaphor is not really intelligible until it is viewed in relation to his philosophical anthropology, where he emphasizes repeatedly the "servile will" as disclosed in the "bound" character of mythic-symbolic discourse. Not only is the symbol *bound*, he says, because it is constituted by a linguistic and nonlinguistic aspect (the nonlinguistic element being so primordial, obscure, and diffuse that it resists all manner of interpretation), but it is also *bound* in the sense that definitive interpretations of symbol naïvely presuppose a grasp on the obscurity limits of human consciousness. Consequently the theorists of the obscurity limits (especially psychologists) have to invent a "hybrid language" that can somehow navigate the aporia between the semantic and the nonsemantic dimensions of experience (the conscious and the unconscious), languages that are usually the combination of an "energetics" (*bios*) and a "semantics" (*logos*).[8]

Metaphorical discourse, by contrast, "is already in the purified universe of *logos*," as Ricoeur puts it, being the product of reflection that represents, as in Turbayne, the conscious manipulation of experience and meaning.[9] Whereas the symbol, for Ricoeur, "hovers on the dividing line between *bios* and *logos*," the metaphor "is the free invention of discourse" and is bound no longer to the archaic images of a sacred cosmos but only to language.[10] This is why for Ricoeur an analysis of metaphor offers a unique opportunity for rendering explicit the semantic structure of symbol in language and partially overcoming, thereby, the obscure character of its reference. The unique power of symbol, on the other hand, is its capacity to point us to the nonlinguistic, nonsemantic roots of experience: "Symbols plunge us into the shadowy experience of power. Metaphors are just the linguistic surface of symbols, and they owe their power to relate the semantic surface to the presemantic surface in the depths of human experience to the two-dimensional structure of the symbol."[11] So it is that the split reference intrinsic to the metaphoric copula has a deeper ground both in the consciousness of the subject and, perhaps, the world and reality as such.

Now the critical question for us here and throughout the remainder of this essay is this: Is the language of boundary and being bounded simply an idiosyncratic feature of being human? Or is the experience of being bounded and the symbolic-metaphoric language that is its consequence ultimately transparent to the nature of reality *per se*? If the former holds true, then it would seem that one cannot finally negotiate the aporia between anthropology and ontology except through divine revelation. But if the latter possibility holds true, then perhaps the language of boundary and split reference can say something not only about being human but also about Being as such. I would like to explore these alternatives by way of Karl Jaspers with respect to the first option and by way of Heidegger with respect to the second, since it seems to me that Ricoeur himself seems to be hovering between these two possibilities with respect to the meaning of metaphorical truth.

There is for me no question that Jaspers' philosophy of *Grenzsituationen* has made a fundamental impact on the philosophy of Ricoeur and that this influence continues to manifest itself in his work on metaphor.[12] Ricoeur, of course, is not alone here, for it was Jaspers' philosophy of boundary situations (first introduced in his *Psychologie der Weltanschauungen* in 1919), as Spiegelberg points out, that was responsible for a new era in European philosophy.[13] Freeing himself, at least partially, from the prevailing currents of neo-Kantianism (which is dubiously labeled "the most threadbare orthodoxy of them all"), Jaspers focused his attention on the concrete situations of man's being-in-a-world and away from strictly formal questions of logic and epistemology. Jaspers' method in this task was phenomenology of the type developed in *Allgemein Psychopathologie* (1913), wherein he challenged the prevailing and highly deterministic neurophysiological categorizations of mental disorders. As a phenomenologist and on the basis of his own extensive experience as a clinical psychiatrist, Jaspers redescribed the apparent permutations of human behavior as they appeared and not from the standpoint of an a priori grasp of normality and abnormality. It was Jaspers' descriptive psychology of understanding (*verstehenden Psychologie*) that provided the basis for his description of "worldviews" in 1919, and it is this approach that was developed formally in *Philosophie* and in his subsequent writings. But as Gadamer notes in his lucid essay on "The Phenomenological Movement," the full impact of Jaspers' formal work in *Philosophie* was short-circuited in its overall impact by the appearance of Heidegger's *Sein und Zeit* in 1926—before Jaspers' work had even gone to press.[14] Nonetheless the spirit of Jaspers' philosophizing *aus möglicher Existenz* continued, and it remained for later thinkers, including Heidegger, Gadamer, and Ricoeur, who was one of his students, to refine the many notions and ideas introduced by Jaspers in a highly literary style.

What then is the *boundary situation* and what does it have to do with Ricoeur's theory of metaphor?

For Jaspers boundary awareness has to do with the subject's gradual discovery of the fundamental limits of knowledge, as in Kant, and an awareness of the degree to which the various projects of human aspiration are riddled with contingency, finitude, and uncertainty, as in Kierkegaard. To use Ricoeur's term, it has to do with the developing awareness of the degree to which man is "bounded" and the radical implications this has for the understanding of both self and world. Boundary awareness for Jaspers, however, also has to do with the awareness of an ineffable, nonobjectifiable dimension of experience before which both the languages of objectivity and subjectivity fail or founder in the face of communicating its possible meaning. This failing or foundering gives rise to a kind of thinking "that begins where cognition ends."[15] This new kind of thinking (in so many ways similar to the kind of thinking called for by Heidegger)[16] is what Jaspers terms "transcending-thinking through the ciphers of speculative metaphysics," or what I here term the symbolic-metaphoric mode of reflection and discourse.

This is not for Jaspers just a theoretical possibility. It is a kind of thinking that arises in the concrete situations of life, especially the *Krisis* situations in which the subject must decide upon a course of action wholly apart from clear knowledge concerning either its origin or goal. The experience of guilt, evil, the tragic, freedom, and fate are all boundary situations, and death is the supreme example since it looms before the subject as the abysmal end of experience and thought. Here the experience of being bounded confronts the subject in all of its terrifying ambiguity, for at the absolute boundary of the known and the unknown we confront a limit that cannot be transcended through the accumulation of more information. Such experiences issue in profoundly disorienting disjunctions as one confronts the "brokenness of Being" (*der Zerrissenheit des Seins*). In Ricoeur's terms this kind of experience produces "semantic shock" and a new "conceptual need" (RM, 296). Boundary awareness can be covered up in the cynicism of everydayness, as Heidegger suggests; it can be the occasion for eternal sedation through the avowal of escapist religious beliefs, as Marx and Neitzsche observed; it can end in madness, as in the case of Hölderlin; or it can result in an authentic conversion which Jaspers calls "the awakening of Existenz" with "Transcendence arising upon its ruins."

In any case, the central point is that the fundamental questions of human existence cannot be answered either on the grounds of the objectifying principles of pure cognition or on the basis of their reduction to the emotive structures of subjectivity. The fundamental questions of being-in-a-world find their elucidation from the boundary alone; it is a situation that is identified with a quest for self-Being that is fundamentally incomplete and openended. This is why Jaspers agrees with Kant that any ontology considered as a definitive doctrine of reality in its totality is impossible and why he works toward the rehabilitation of metaphysics as "authentic philosophizing on the basis of possible Existenz." Ontology, then, is redefined as *periechontology*, or an ontology of active sufferance that circles round the way of Being, so to speak, and that it is always, as in Ricoeur, "the second to the last word."

The difference between Jaspers and Ricoeur has precisely to do with the character of the presumed *last word* and what can be salvaged in the face of this limit. For Jaspers the last word and its meaning is perceived indirectly through a "thinking ascertain-

ment" of boundary situations in which the subject or self is able
"to break through mundane existence" by reading experience and
world now become the "ciphers of Transcendence."[17] For Ricoeur
this last word seems to be *metaphorical,* through which we see
"that most primordial, most hidden dialectic" (RM, 313) but beyond or behind which we cannot go. As such it is very strictly
speaking "the second to the last word," with Jaspers' claims regarding transcendence-Itself being viewed as the product of subjective inference. Indeed, Ricoeur has characterized Jaspers'
"reverential love for the hidden Transcendence" as "lyricism juxtaposed with unreconciled tragedy" and declared that his position leads finally to a "disquieting aestheticism" in which *amor
fati* and not Transcendence has the "final word."[18]

The subject or self (*mögliche Existenz*) in Jaspers' view,
however, is not a fixed but a "moving center," and traditional
conceptions of the transcendental ego are thereby displaced.
"There is," Jaspers insists, "no totality of the 'I am,' for the self is
always more than I can know."[19] To put it another way, the self
considered as possible Existenz is always viewed by Jaspers as an
"encompassing" dialectically grounded in the "Encompassing"
that the self is not. Therefore when he suggests that "Transcendence rises upon the ruins of Existenz," it is not the self *per se* that
is the ground of Being but rather *Freedom.* Indeed, the term
Freedom for Jaspers is the ultimate symbol or metaphor, for in it
the referential aspects of Transcendence and the Encompassing
coalesce and disappear. As such, Freedom cannot really be
viewed as the ultimate ground of either the self or Being but more
accurately as an absence of ground or an abyss as in the *Ungrund*
or *Abgrund* of the mystics. Nevertheless, it is here that Being
touches us most concretely. We may attempt to describe it in metaphor, symbol, or any other manner of speech, but even then, as
in the case of Job's encounter with the Whirlwind, it is as though
we were saying nothing, "Words in a silence that will not break."

Thus for Jaspers as for Ricoeur there is no ontology "ready
made" (RM, 295) in metaphor. But for Jaspers this second to the
last word *is* the last word insofar as it can be spoken, that is, for
him the authentic ciphers of Transcendence are as fathomless as
the Freedom to which they are transparent. In the face of such an

abyss we must be content with philosophizing on the grounds of possible Existenz (*aus möglicher Existenz*) that is itself an ontology of "active sufferance." But in Ricoeur there are signs that this is not enough. Indeed, Ricoeur's earlier work, as we have pointed out in relation to Jaspers, may be viewed as an attempt to adumbrate rather radically the voluntarism he sees present to existential phenomenology, an adumbration that takes place through very careful and detailed attention to what it means to be an incarnate and an affective, and not just a willing and a thinking, subject. Nevertheless, Ricoeur's tensive theory of metaphorical truth still seems to be grounded in the self nonidentical with itself as we have shown, and it is this *boundary* or hiatus between the self and itself that seems to be the reflective occasion for the split reference in metaphorical predication. But what is the *beyond* to which it refers *at center*, so to speak? It was the mystic theologian Cusanus who spoke at great length about experience and knowledge become a "coincidence of opposites" (*coincidentia oppositorum*) through all manner of philosophical reflection. Nevertheless he asserted that "Thou, O Lord, art beyond the wall of the coincidence of opposites!" How could he know this? Is this the language of faith—what Gadamer and Pannenberg refer to as religious or doxological speaking—and to be distinguished categorically from all manner of rational speaking, even metaphorical speaking? Is it precisely here that we encounter the limits of hermeneutic philosophy as a facilitating device for speculative metaphysics? Or do we here encounter the limits of the Ricoeurean model and the necessity for an even more radical break with the neo-Kantian tradition that informs not only Ricoeur but Cassirer and Jaspers as well? We cannot hope to answer these questions here, but they will serve as a general horizon for my final comments in the remaining section.

HERMENEUTIC PHILOSOPHY
AND THE PROBLEM OF ONTOLOGY

I have suggested that Ricoeur seems to believe that the rehabilitation of Western metaphysics is closely related to the development of an imaginative but critical philosophy of metaphor. For this to be accomplished, however, he must come to terms with Heidegger, and Heidegger for Ricoeur clearly presents a problem. Throughout his writings (especially those authored since 1960) Ricoeur has indicated many times that he is at once attracted to and repulsed by the philosophy of Heidegger. In the final study of *The Rule of Metaphor* we are again confronted with what might be termed a *dual* reading of Heidegger. On the one hand, Ricoeur recognizes that Heidegger cannot be avoided in view of the stated intentions of his own poetics of Transcendence. It is Heidegger, after all, who more than anyone else in recent history has turned to language as the "house of Being" and the place where Transcendence is gathered. On the other hand, Ricoeur has stated repeatedly that what he calls Heidegger's "direct route to Being" is not for him.

Ricoeur's refusal seems to stem from two basic motives. First, he refused to accept the implications of what he terms Heidegger's "vengeful" indictment of Western metaphysics. He simply does not agree that Western philosophy lost its bearings with the shift from *mythos* (in the pre-Socratics) to *logos* (in Plato and Aristotle). Thus he rejects the notion that "the trans-gression (*Über-tragung*) of the meta-phor and the trans-gression of metaphysics are one and the same transfer" (RM, 280) and that the metaphorical, as Heidegger contends, "can exist only within the metaphysical." To be sure, metaphorical discourse for Ricoeur represents a transition to *logos*, but it is an ambiguous shift due to the paradoxical character of the "is/is not" metaphoric copula which places before us, in some instances, the antecedent ground of symbol. However, it is the peculiar mode of metaphoric predication that is of decisive importance for Ricoeur in the understanding of metaphor and *not* the grasping of some pure-primordial ontology that is hidden within metaphor and that is on the verge of being lost. Consequently Ricoeur is not interested in the direct route of the Heideggerian retrieval (*Wiederholen*) of the ancient name of Being through the development of "a thinking that recalls" (*andenkendes Denken*) Being in its "forgetfulness," a thinking which, for Ricoeur, must abandon the linguistic sciences, epistemology, and even discourse itself. He is interested rather in the elucidation of the intersection of the two separate spheres of discourse present to a given metaphorical network and how in the larger view one can understand metaphorical discourse and philosophical speculation in a complementary and mutually enhancing manner. So it is, Ricoeur insists against Heidegger, "that it is not metaphor that carries the structure of Platonic metaphysics; metaphysics rather seizes the metaphorical process in order to make it work to the benefit of metaphysics" (RM, 294–295). To adopt the Heideggerian perspective, he says, is to succumb to a "fascination with the fecundity of oblivion" (RM, 291) or, as he puts it elsewhere, to be seduced by "romanticisms of the always anterior."

Ricoeur, secondly, seems to identify the goal of Heidegger's ontology with an immediate-immediate that can be known intuitively through the cultivation of something akin to pure experience. Against what we might here also term the "obscurity limit" represented in Heidegger, Ricoeur holds out for the gradualistic processes of *mediation* and the necessary work of the *concept* as in Hegel. One must not, Ricoeur insists, opt for the "mystification of primitive sense," a position "that would ultimately leave discourse behind" and lead to "hermeticism" and "affectedness" (RM, 313). Such an option, he says, "invites us to sever discourse from its propositional character, forgetting Hegel's lesson that even speculative propositions never cease to be propositions" (RM, 313).

But is Heidegger the "affected hermeticist" that Ricoeur here suggests? Or is there an aspect of Heidegger—fundamentally and originally dialectical—that Ricoeur has overlooked? Does Heidegger represent the "choice between Athens and Jerusalem," as Ricoeur puts it, or between Nietzsche and Kierkegaard that some have thought to be the case? Or is there a dimension of Heidegger's *piety* that we have not really understood and which makes him less inimical to Christianity? The recent surge of studies into the religious dimension of Heidegger would suggest that earlier commentaries do not have the final word on Heidegger's problematical relationship with Christianity.[20] One scarcely needs to mention that there have been similar shifts with respect to the interpretation of Nietzsche, interpretations which greatly depend, obviously, on what one understands Christianity itself to be in the first place.

With respect to the question of dialectic it is Gadamer who

has pointed out that for Heidegger it was always Hegel who presented the preeminent challenge; that the overcoming (*Überwindung*) of metaphysics in Heidegger has not only the Nietzschean quality of negation (*aufgehoben*) but also the Hegelian aspect of a "getting over" through a "coming to terms with" (*Verwinden*) that is creative sublimation (*Aufhebung*).[21] It is with this fully in view that Gadamer asks the difficult question as to how we may finally position Heidegger with respect to Hegel. Do we place him, as he puts it, on the fringes with other neo-Kantians like Husserl and Jaspers, or is Heidegger's "interrogation" of Hegel so radical that "he leaves out nothing which Hegel asks and at the same time asks more deeply than Hegel and therefore has gotten behind him?"[22] In Hegel, Gadamer points out, "reason's universal power of synthesis is not only able to mediate the oppositions in thought, but also is able to sublimate the oppositions in the real world. It demonstrates exactly this in history insofar as the most alien, inscrutable and inimical forces of history are surmounted by reason's power of reconciliation. Reason is reconciliation with ruination."[23] While Ricoeur does not extend the Hegelian *Aufhebung* to the historical process, it is certainly implicit in the general character of his hermeneutics and his tensive theory of metaphor, in which, as he puts it, a new "semantic pertinence" arises out of the "ruins of impertinent predication" as the sphere of discourse known as speculative philosophy does its conceptual work.

For Heidegger, on the other hand, "the conceptual mediation of every conceivable path of thought" itself belies the attempt to "break out" of the "circle of reflection."[24] In Gadamer's view it would seem that it is precisely the process Ricoeur outlines that leads to the "forgetfulness of Being"; in other words, it is conceptual mediation that stands in the way of truly hearing what Heidegger out of Angelus Silesius calls "the blossoming forth" of "words like flowers" (RM, 308–309). As a result the primordial *logos*—which Heidegger identifies originally with the verb *legein*, "to lay down" or "to lay before"[25]—is transmuted into an *eidos*; the being-in-the-neighborhood-of-Being that is a *hearing* of Being's call is transformed into another transcendental perception of beings controlled by the ego's re-presentative and re-productive powers of mediation. Thus it is precisely *because* Heidegger has thought through dialectic to a foundational level that Heidegger, according to Gadamer, "is not oriented towards speaking as it occurs in the form of a statement, but rather towards the temporalness of the presence itself which speaks to us, saying it is always more a holding true to the whole of what is to be said and a holding back before what is unsaid."[26]

Ricoeur demonstrates, to be sure, that Heidegger himself is keenly aware of the dynamics of the intersection of the spheres of poetical and philosophical discourse. This is why Ricoeur suggests that we have far more to learn from the manner in which Heidegger "constantly uses metaphor" than from what "he says in passing against metaphor" (RM, 280). What is fundamentally different, however, is that Heidegger refuses to develop even the possibility of an ontology of metaphor based upon this intersection. To do so would be to slip back into "re-presentational" thinking and to extend hermeneutic philosophizing beyond its limits by transforming it into yet another philosophy *of* language.

And is it not, in fact, just the implied *use* of metaphor that is at the heart of the problem here? It is Ricoeur and not Heidegger who speaks of the felicitous *deployment* of metaphor as a means of vivifying language and, by implication, speculative metaphysics as it responds to the semantic innovations of metaphorical discourse. At the obvious level, of course, we all use metaphor just as we use other aspects of language. Here Ricoeur has indeed clearly indicated the difference between the dead or lexicalized and the living metaphor. But as Gadamer has shown out of Heidegger, the most fundamental and by far the most difficult lesson we have to learn about language is, not how we use it, but rather how language *uses us*. Only then, he insists, will we be in a position to understand just what it is that "language speaks" or "gives." It is just this awareness of the preformative power of language, history, and tradition that for Gadamer is fundamental to any possible *demontage* of the subject-object problem of post-Kantian epistemology and philosophies of the subject as the key to Being— whether they are elaborated in terms of mind, will, or feeling. It would seem, therefore, that apart from a willingness to entertain seriously the extremities of Heidegger's *turn* from the conceptual mediation of meaning it is impossible to appreciate the meaning of his contention that "language is the clearing-and-concealing event of Being-itself."[27]

Professor Carl Raschke, I think, has placed this extremity rather squarely before us in a recent article on Heidegger and "The End of Theology." In his provocative essay he suggests that the "meditative" thinking of Heidegger "demands of the theologian unconditional and fateful humility in his formulation of a response to the holy, a humility which is perhaps too severe and taxing for theological professionals to bear."[28] While this statement may be a bit excessive as a wholesale indictment, it does effectively bring into focus what I would like to develop briefly as the mystical character of Heidegger's *renunciation* of all manner of objectifying thinking including hermeneutics or any new method of nonobjectifying thinking.

While renunciation in Heidegger is not wholly unlike Ricoeur's *refusal* of the direct route to ontology, it is different in the following way. In Ricoeur refusal has more of a formal character informed, as it is, by eschatology considered as a limiting principle both epistemologically and theologically. In the face of such a principle all claims to an "absolute transcendence of the cave" are for Ricoeur both uncritical and the sign of *hubris*. Philosophical idealism and its offspring voluntaristic existentialism have for Ricoeur this Promethean quality generally.[29]

But Heidegger's renunciation, while it too is informed by a critical refusal in the face of the temptations of mind, is more akin, at a deeper level, to the care-full resolve that guides the life choice of the contemplative. Indeed, Heidegger, more than any other recent thinker, is the one who has, in his own circuitous way, reawakened Westerners to the meaning of renunciation in its philosophical dimension. Since the Protestant Reformation (and we must here recall the Roman Catholic background of Heidegger) renunciation has itself been renounced and largely expunged as a virtuous aspect of piety. Indeed, renunciation is identified of late only with *sannyasi* of the Orient and is viewed as something fundamentally inappropriate to "worldly" Christianity. But now we are beginning to see that renunciation, as it is manifest in medieval thinkers like John Scotus Erigena, Meister

Eckhart, Cusanus, and John of the Cross, may have an epistemological cogency that transcends considerably the charge of its being worldless escapism. What we see, rather, is the kind of renunciation that is implicit in the warning of the Pseudo-Dionysius
when he enjoined his readers by saying, "Think not that by ordinary knowing you can know Him who has made the dark His
hiding place!" It is precisely this kind of renunciation to which
Heidegger alludes in his oft-quoted line from Stefan George:
"And so I renounced and sadly see / Where word breaks off no
thing may be."[30] Here renunciation has to do with a standing-
silent before that which language holds in its *reserve*: the "twilit-
boundary-situation" in which "the poetic saying borders on the
fateful source of speech."[31] For Heidegger this renunciation is *ecstatic* in the worldly and not otherworldly sense precisely because
it is the acceptance of a call to "stand-in" rather than to "stand-
out," that is, an "open-standing" or "standing-in the unconcealed-
ness of Being, from Being, in Being."[32]

Such a "way back to the ground of metaphysics" sounds very
strange to many Western ears. But this is not surprising when we
begin to appreciate the degree to which we are wholly the captives of transcendental philosophies of reflection, philosophies
that are, in turn, based upon temporalized conceptions of the
self. Some of the more recent studies on the subject of the self,
however, indicate a break with this approach and are moving to
relational-process models of psychology and metaphysics in order
to focus more radically upon experien*cing* rather than reflecting
on the meaning of experience. Paradoxical as this may sound, it is
an approach that draws its support not only from modern physics
(informed by quantum and relativity theory) but also from Buddhist philosophers like Nishida Kitaro and the Christian mystic
Meister Eckhart. In a statement that comes very close to the Buddhist *Ānatta*, or "no self" doctrine, Harold Oliver maintains that
for Eckhart the attainment of genuine humility depends on "getting beyond time" and the assumed fundamentality that time
plays in egoic conceptions of the self. For Eckhart this means, as
Oliver puts it, that "genuine poverty cannot be an act of the will."
Quoting from Eckhart he says:

As long as one wills to do the will of God, and yearns for eternity and God, one is not really poor [i.e., "fully renounced"]; for he who is poor wills nothing, knows nothing, wants nothing.[33]

Heidegger's remarkable "Dialogue on Language" with the unnamed Japanese philosopher (who is, it seems, a student of Nishida Kitaro) presupposes a similar common understanding with respect to the renunciation of the temporalized self and the comprehension of *no-things* that *are* where "the word breaks up." Here Heidegger and his friend ponder the utter inadequacy of language conceived in terms of *sense* and *reference* as a corollary that can elucidate the "two-fold," namely, the "presentness of what is present."[34] This *presentness* is something that can only be *hinted* at by the "bearer of language," namely, by the one "who walks on the boundary of the boundless."[35] It is, moreover, a presentness that is given only in dialogue and *between* those who have renounced objectifying theories of language. It is precisely this disposition to renunciation that informs one of Heidegger's rare quotations of Scripture (which he elsewhere refers to as "the Book of books"[36]): "Has not God," he says after Saint Paul, "let the wisdom of the world become foolishness?" "When," he continues, "will Christian theology make up its mind to take seriously the word of the apostle and thus also the conception of philosophy as foolishness?"[37] The foolishness to which Heidegger alludes, of course, is the onto-theology that has emerged with the troubled synthesis of Hebrew spirituality and Hellenistic philosophy during the past two thousand years. But at a deeper level Heidegger's lament is informed by Hölderlin's utterance when, upon his encounter with "the high ones," he says "foolish is my speech"[38]— foolish because it would be "unseemly" here to attempt to express, as Stefan George warns, the *is* that "arises where the word breaks off." It is precisely this kind of renunciation that Heidegger presupposes when he says that "the breaking up of the word is the true step back on the way of thinking."[39]

Ricoeur, as we have seen, regards this as a kind of mystical obscurantism that he cannot accept and feels that it leads ultimately to the despair he sees underlying Wittgenstein's famous

aphorisms at the end of the *Tractatus* (RM, 312). Without press-
ing the issue as to whether or not Ricoeur's assessment of Wittgenstein is accurate, we may simply ask, What are the options? On
the one hand, Ricoeur would avoid the skeptical consequences of
thoroughgoing nominalism, and it would seem that his attention
to metaphor is for this very purpose. But on the other hand, he
cannot abide Heidegger's renunciation of conceptual mediation
for the indirect discourse of *Anwesenheit* and *Gelassenheit*. Thus
it is his intention to remain more public than Heidegger through
the development of a tensive theory of metaphorical truth that
will facilitate the development of an ontology informed by what
he terms the "relative pluralism" of language games (RM, 257).
Does this mean (and here we can only speculate) that Ricoeur is
moving in the direction of "regional ontologies" in the sense suggested by Husserl? But it may also mean that Ricoeur is moving in
the direction of a process metaphysics, as David Pellauer has recently suggested.[40] Indeed, process philosophy is one of the few
subjects that Ricoeur has not as yet explored at any length. It is
difficult to see, however, how process metaphysics will serve the
more orthodox and traditional Christian sentiments of Ricoeur,
especially the problem of transcendence which is to be the subject
of his "Poetics of the Will."

A third possibility may be that Ricoeur simply has not as yet
fully appropriated the implications of that "most primordial—
most primitive dialectic" to which he claims metaphorical utterances are transparent. On its face, after all, this seems to be
basically a transcendental-anthropological conclusion and not
something that can readily accommodate a Christian theology of
revelation. It is not, however, a disclosure without consequence
in relation to either a Buddhist ontology or to the most sublime
examples of Christian mysticism, for in these contexts the dialectic to which Ricoeur alludes points to a common ground that is
both shared and presupposed by all religious metaphysics. In Heidegger's concept of "truth as primordial" (*Alētheia*) we encounter
a thinker who has both recognized the *fate* implicit in such a notion and accepted it. But it is an avowal that becomes *fated* only
insofar as one wishes "to have one's cake and eat it too," that is,
only insofar as one persists in attempting to speak about Being as

we speak of beings. It is for this very reason that Heidegger, sens-
ing the limits of hermeneutic philosophizing, abandons hermeneutics as a method of ontological elucidation and why Jaspers,
too, was suspicious of hermeneutics.

Finally, it is important to note that the primordiality of
Truth in Heidegger must not be confused with primordiality in
the archaic sense, as in Jung. For Heidegger, Being's Truth simply *is*, and temporal references *only* have to do with the subject
and not the character of Being as such. It is for this reason that the
question of *reference* ultimately breaks down once the region of
ontology is broached, just as it breaks down in the theology of the
deus absconditus. As the Buddhist philosopher says to Heidegger,
"For us emptiness is the loftiest name for what you [Westerners]
say with the word Being,"[41] so also can Heidegger reply that Being has to do "with an origin that always comes to meet us from
the future."[42] Thus we are left with the perplexing but not altogether unproductive situation of being attentive to the ontological *question* of Plotinus, "What is this One that does not exist?"
and also of recognizing its fundamental impropriety by listening
to the metaphoric *saying* of Being in a poet like Hölderlin: "That
which thou seekest is near / And already coming to greet thee."[43]

NOTES

1. This work was first published as *La métaphore vive* (Paris:
Éditions du Seuil, 1975) and brought into English translation by Robert
Czerny under the somewhat curious title *The Rule of Metaphor* (Toronto: University of Toronto Press, 1977). I say "curious" because the
word 'rule' clearly detracts from the force of what Ricoeur asserts to be
the *power* of the "living" or "vibrant" metaphor in the creation of meaning. All subsequent references to this work will be cited in parentheses
as RM.

2. See Ernst Cassirer, *Language and Myth*, tr. Suzanne Langer
(New York: Dover, 1946).

3. Ibid., pp. 90–92.

4. Martin Heidegger, *Kant and the Problem of Metaphysics*, tr.
James Churchill (Bloomington: University of Indiana Press, 1962),
p. 173. The original lectures for this text were given in 1929.

5. Ibid., pp. 169–170, 201–202.

6. Elizabeth Sewell, *The Human Metaphor* (Notre Dame: University of Notre Dame Press, 1964), p. 77.

7. Ibid., pp. 200–202. The noted British philosopher-novelist Iris Murdoch sees the matter in a similar way: "Philosophy needs metaphor and metaphor is basic; how basic is the most basic question of them all," and "Metaphors are not merely peripheral decorations or even useful models. They are fundamental forms of our awareness of our condition." *The Fire and the Sun: Why Plato Banished the Artists* (London: Oxford University Press, 1977), p. 88, and *The Sovereignty of Good* (London: Routledge and Kegan Paul, 1970), p. 77.

8. Paul Ricoeur, *Interpretation Theory: Discourse and the Surplus of Meaning* (Fort Worth: Texas Christian University Press, 1975), p. 58.

9. Ibid., p. 59.

10. Ibid., p. 61.

11. Ibid., p. 69.

12. See my *Transcendence and Hermeneutics* (The Hague: Martinus Nijhoff, 1979), pp. 156–169.

13. Herbert Spiegelberg, *Phenomenology and Psychiatry: A Historical Introduction* (Evanston: Northwestern University Press, 1972), pp. 96, 191.

14. Hans-Georg Gadamer, *Philosophical Hermeneutics*, tr. David Linge (Berkeley and Los Angeles: University of California Press, 1976), pp. 136–141.

15. Karl Jaspers, *Philosophy*, 3 vols., tr. E. B. Ashton (Chicago: University of Chicago Press, 1971), 3:3–32. Jaspers' *Philosophie* was originally published in 1932.

16. See *What Is Called Thinking?* (New York: Harper and Row, 1972).

17. Jaspers, *Philosophy*, 2:9 and 2:175–192.

18. Paul Schilpp, ed., *The Philosophy of Karl Jaspers* (New York: Tudor, 1957), pp. 615, 617, 633–639. See also Ricoeur's studies of Jaspers entitled *Gabriel Marcel et Karl Jaspers: Philosophie du mystère et philosophie du paradoxe* (Paris, 1948) and, with Mikel Dufrenne, *Karl Jaspers et la philosophie de l'existence* (Paris, 1947). These are Ricoeur's first two published works of book length.

19. Jaspers, *Philosophy*, 2:33.

20. See, for example, James Perotti, *Heidegger on the Divine* (Athens: Ohio University Press, 1974), and John Caputo, *The Mystical Element in Heidegger's Thought* (Athens: Ohio University Press, 1978).

There is a considerable distance between these works and Walter Kaufmann's assessment of Heidegger as an "atheist" in the 1950s.

21. Hans-Georg Gadamer, *Hegel's Dialectic: Five Hermeneutical Studies*, tr. P. Christopher Smith (New Haven: Yale University Press, 1976), p. 100.

22. Ibid., p. 103.

23. Ibid., p. 105.

24. Ibid., pp. 101–102.

25. See Martin Heidegger, *Early Greek Thinking* (New York: Harper and Row, 1975), especially the essay on "Logos" (Heraclitus, Fragment B 50), pp. 59–78.

26. Gadamer, *Hegel's Dialectic*, p. 115.

27. See Martin Heidegger's "Letter on Humanism," in *Philosophy in the Twentieth Century*, vol. 3, ed. William Barrett and Henry Aiken (New York: Random House, 1962), p. 279.

28. Karl Raschke, "The End of Theology," *Journal of the American Academy of Religion* 46:2 (June 1978): 173.

29. Paul Ricoeur, *Freedom and Nature: The Voluntary and the Involuntary*, tr. Erazim Kohak (Evanston: Northwestern University Press, 1966), p. 464.

30. Martin Heidegger, *On the Way to Language*, tr. Peter Hertz (New York: Harper and Row, 1971), p. 67.

31. Ibid., pp. 67–69.

32. See Martin Heidegger's "On the Way Back to the Ground of Metaphysics," in Barrett and Aiken, *Philosophy in the Twentieth Century*, pp. 206–218.

33. Harold H. Oliver, unpublished paper entitled "Western Introspection and the Temporalization of the Will," delivered before the Boston Theological Society in October 1978. For a more complete understanding of Oliver's position on this and related matters see "The Complementarity of Theology and Cosmology," *Zygon: Journal of Religion and Science* 13:1 (March 1978): 19–33; "Theses on the Relational Self and the Genesis of the Western Ego," *Theologische Zeitschrift* 33 (September–October 1977): 326–335; and Professor Oliver's essay above.

34. Heidegger, *On the Way to Language*, pp. 15, 34.

35. Ibid., p. 41.

36. Ibid., p. 10.

37. Heidegger, "On the Way Back to the Ground of Metaphysics," in Barrett and Aiken, *Philosophy in the Twentieth Century*, p. 216.

38. Heidegger, *Existence and Being*, ed. Werner Brock (Chicago:

Regnery, 1949), especially "Remembrance of the Poet" and "Hölderlin and the Essence of Poetry," pp. 233–291.

39. Heidegger, *On the Way to Language*, p. 108.

40. See David Pellauer's response to Gary Madison's "Reflections on Paul Ricoeur's Philosophy of Metaphor," in *Philosophy Today* 21:4 (Winter 1977): 437–445.

41. Heidegger, *On the Way to Language*, p. 19.

42. Ibid., p. 10.

43. Heidegger, *Existence and Being*, p. 224.

PART III

Interpretations of Myth

8

The Spoken Word and the Work of Interpretation in American Indian Religion

DENNIS TEDLOCK

OUR TEXT COMES FROM THE Aashiwi, as they call them-selves, or from the Zuni Indians. They live in a town in west-central New Mexico and are now twice as numerous as they were when the Spanish first counted them in 1540. Their language is *shiwi'ma*,[1] one of the 150 languages spoken by the various indige-nous peoples of the United States.

The name of the text is *chimiky'ana'kowa*. Literally trans-lated, that means "that which was the beginning." It *is* the begin-ning, or "that which *was* the beginning." These words were made by what happened at the beginning, and to tell these words is to happen the beginning again. *Chimiky'ana'kowa*.

I speak of a *text*, even though the Zunis do not have a *manu-script* of the beginning. But there is a way of fixing *words* without making visible *marks*. As with alphabetic writing, this fixing is done by a *radical simplification* of ordinary talk. Ordinary talk not only has words, in the sense of strings of consonants and vow-els, but it has patterns of stress, of emphasis, of pitch, of tone, of pauses or stops that can move somewhat independently of the sheer words and make the "same" words mean quite different things or even the opposite of what they started out to mean.[2] To *fix a text* without making *visible marks* is to bring *stress* and *pitch* and *pause* into a fixed relationship with the *words*. The Zunis call this *ana k'eyato'u*, "raising it right up," and we would call it chant. In Zuni chant a strong stress and a high, gliding pitch come into concert on the last syllable of each phrase, or sometimes at the end of a single important word, and are immediately followed by a deliberate silence. All other, weaker stresses occurring between two pauses are equal, and all lower pitches are resolved into a monotone.[3] The number of syllables between two pauses varies from around six or seven to twenty or more. This variation has the effect of giving emphasis to the shortest lines, but this is an emphasis *fixed* in the *text* rather than being left to the voice of an individual speaker on a particular occasion. It all sounds something like this (try a monotone chant, with strong stress and a quick rise on each line-final syllable):[4]

> Nomilhte ho'n chimiky'anapkya teya
> awiten tehwula
> annohsiyan tehwula
> ho'na liilha aateyaye. . . .

> Now in truth our beginning is:
> the fourth inner world
> the soot inner world
> is where we live. . . .

The words, or rather the word, of the *chimiky'ana'kowa*, "that which was the beginning," is fixed in a text called *Kyaklo 'an penanne*, the Word of Kyaklo.[5] Kyaklo is a person, a Zuni, who witnessed some of the events of the beginning. He comes once each four or eight years to give his word. He is a stubborn, cranky cripple who must be carried everywhere he goes by the clowns who accompany him, and he always demands that the smallest one do it. He always comes into town by the same path, the same path he has followed since the beginning. There is a new subdivision whose streets do not follow his path, so he must be carried through people's yards. There is a house that sits in his path, so he must be carried up over the roof and down the other side. When they come to the river, just before entering the old part of town, he insists that the clowns wade through the ice and mud of the river rather than taking the bridge. They always manage to drop him with all his fine clothes. Kyaklo's face is bordered by the rainbow and the milky way, and rain falls from his eyes and mouth. All he does, besides chanting, is to call out his own name: "Kyaklo Kyaklo Kyaklo Kyaklo." The people who want to hear his word assemble in six different ceremonial chambers, or *kivas*.[6] He carries a duck in his right hand, and if anyone falls asleep while he talks, he hits them with the duck's bill. He goes from one building to the next, still chanting even while being carried through the streets; no one person hears the whole word on one occasion, except for the clowns who carry him. On top of that, he uses a lot of arcane and esoteric vocabulary, so that those who are not well versed in such matters have difficulty in following. Worse than that, he chants rather fast and his words are muffled by his mask. To wear Kyaklo's mask a person must devote his whole life, for one year, to studying for the part.

So there is our text. Like a cleanly alphabetic text, it consists of a sheer string of words. Kyaklo always pronounces the same words in the same way; it is always Kyaklo chanting, not a particular wearer of the mask. There are no shifts of stress or pitch or pause to find a new meaning, to say nothing of a search for different *words*. Such is the nature of what we call "authoritative texts": they go on saying exactly the same thing, over and over, forever. Any way you look at it, Kyaklo is authoritative text personified.

Now, the *interpretation* of the *chimiky'ana'kowa*, "that which was the beginning," is another matter. The story does not end with Kyaklo. There are fourteen priesthoods at Zuni charged with meditation on the weather and with divination, and each of them has an interpretation of the beginning.[7] There are thirteen medicine societies charged with curing, and each of them has an interpretation. And in every Zuni household there is at least one parent or grandparent who knows how to interpret the beginning. I say "interpretation" partly because these are not fixed texts. The stresses, pitches, pauses, and also the *sheer words* are different from one interpreter to the next, and even from one occasion to the next, according to the place and time, according to who is in the audience, according to what they do or do not already know, according to what questions they may have asked, even according to what may happen, outside the events of the narrative itself, during this particular telling.[8] Or the interpreter may suddenly realize something or understand something for the first time on this particular occasion. The teller is not merely repeating memorized words, nor is he or she merely giving a dramatic "oral interpretation" or "concert reading" of a fixed script. We are in the presence of a *performing art*, all right, but we are getting the *criticism* at the same time and from the same person. The interpreter does not merely play the parts but is the narrator and commentator as well. What we are hearing is the *hermeneutics* of the text of Kyaklo. At times we may hear direct quotations from that text, but they are embedded in a hermeneutics.

Now, our own phenomenologists and structuralists also quote their texts, removing words from context and even daring to insert their own *italics*: "Italics mine." But there is a difference here: the interpreter of that which was the beginning must keep the *story* going. And in this process the storyteller-interpreter does not merely quote or paraphrase the text but may even *improve* upon it, describe a scene which it does not describe, or answer a question which it does not answer.

The Word of Kyaklo, taken by itself, is a sacred object, a relic. It is not a visible or tangible object, but it is an object nevertheless. What we hear from our interpreter is simultaneously something new *and* a comment on that relic, both a restoration and a further possibility. I emphasize this point because ethnologists down to the present day have hankered after the sacred object itself whenever they could get their hands on it, while devaluing what I am here calling "interpretations." Dell Hymes falls into this pattern when he makes a distinction between what he calls "a *telling about* the story" and "a *doing of* the story" (italics mine).[9] He suggests that we need to gather up the "true performances" from our collections of North American narratives, sorting these out from the mere "tellings," or "reportings," which exist in these same collections. What is stark about this position is that it leaves the "telling about" the story, including commentary and interpretation, entirely up to the ethnologist, while the proper business of the native is limited to the "doing of" the story. This is close to the position of the French structuralists, who limit the native to a narrative or "diachronic" function and concede exclusive rights to the analytic or "synchronic" function to themselves. In effect, the collected texts are treated as if they were raw products, to which value is then added by manufacture.

For the Zuni storyteller-interpreter the relationship between text and interpretation is a dialectical one: he or she both respects the text and revises it. For the ethnologist that relationship is a dualistic opposition. In the end the text remains the text, still there in the archives and still waiting to be brought to light; the analysis remains the analysis, bearing no resemblance *to* the text and learning nothing *from* the text, and the analyst even takes professional pride in that fact.

The interpretation of the Kyaklo text that concerns us here was given by a man named Andrew Peynetsa, then sixty-two-years old, at his farmhouse in the evening.[10] Checking my notes, I find that he gave this narrative thirteen years ago last Sunday and finished it thirteen years ago today, on March 29, 1965. He was talking to his wife, one of his sons, his brother, and myself. I, of course, had a tape recorder, and my translation from the Zuni follows not only the original words but also the original loudnesses, softnesses, tones, and silences.

Andrew, as a boy, had heard the entire Word of Kyaklo. He and a cousin had been pestering their grandfather to tell a tale, the kind of story the Zunis tell for entertainment. Their grandfather was a cranky old man who did not really know any tales, but one night he finally consented to tell them something. It turned out to be the Word of Kyaklo. He kept them awake all night, hitting them with a stick whenever they nodded. At dawn he sent them out to do their chores. The next night he resumed his talk, going on all night again. And so on for another night and another, finishing at dawn on the fourth day.

The Zuni beginning does not begin with a first cause; it does not derive an infinite chain of dualisms from a first dualism that in turn springs from original absolute oneness. When the story opens, the earth is already here, the *awitelin tsitta*, literally the "four-chambered mother." There are four more worlds under this one, darker and darker. In this room we are on the third floor, so the bottommost world beneath this one would be a secret base-

ment below the actual basement of this building.[11] Only the Sun
Father is up here in this world. Four stories beneath in the Soot
Room, in total darkness, are the people. The problem is, not to
create human beings, but to have them up here in this world,
making prayers and offerings to the Sun Father and receiving his
daylight, his life. The people down in the fourth room beneath
are only *moss people*: they have webbed feet, webbed hands, tails
of moss; they are slimy. They do not know what fire is, or lightning, or daylight, or even dawn.

In the Word of Kyaklo and in all previously recorded interpretations the three rooms between this world and the Soot Room
are apparently vacant.[12] This is where Andrew's interpretation
introduces one of its elaborations or improvements:[13]

At the beginning
When the earth was still soft
the first people came out
the ones who had been living in the first room beneath.
When they came out they made their villages
they made their houses a——ll around the land.

So the first people out were not ourselves, as in the other versions,
but people who were living in the first room beneath this one. But
the Sun Father was displeased because "they did not think of anything": they did not give prayers and offerings. When the people
in the second room came out, their sulphurous smell, their ozone
smell, killed all the first ones. They in turn did not think of anything. The people from the third room beneath came out, and
their sulphurous smell killed the second people, and they, too, did
not think of anything.

The idea that three unsuccessful approximations of human
beings preceded ourselves is a common one among Mesoamerican
peoples, far to the south of the Zunis. But it is not our concern
here to pretend to "explain" the source, the origin, of this part of
the present narrative. The point is that Kyaklo leaves three rooms
vacant, and our interpreter fills them. This may be something
"new," or it may even be a restoration of something that Kyaklo
forgot. Whatever the case, these first three peoples live and die in
a storyteller's *interpretation* and not in the chanter's *text*. They
are *not* in the "book."

As we heard before, these previous people "made their villages a——ll around the land." Our interpreter stops for a moment to comment on this:

Their ruins are all around the land as you can see.
Around the mountains where there is no water today, you
    could get water just by pulling up a clump of grass
because the earth was soft.
This is the way they lived, there at the beginning.

Not only is this a departure from the official text; it is a departure from the "doing of" the story, and it changes over from third person narrative to direct address: "as *you* can see." Interpretation, here in the form of a small lecture, is in the very *midst* of the *text*. It happens again just a few lines later, as the narrator leads us toward the moment when the twin sons of the Sun Father come into existence. It had been raining all night:

Where there were waterfalls
the water made foam.
Well, you know how water can make foam
certainly
it can make foam

certainly
that water
made suds.

It was there
where the suds were made
that the two Bow Priests
sprouted.

There the two Ahayuuta
received life.
Their father brought them to life:
they came out of the suds.

And in another place, having told an episode in which Nepayatamu, the patron of the Clown Society, brings the Molaawe, or corn deities, back into the town after a famine, our interpreter comments:

When the Molaawe enter today
the same procedure is followed:
Nepayatamu
does not speak
when he enters
and the priests are completely quiet inside, well, you
have seen this yourself, at the kiva.

Such passages as these raise questions about the relationship of
text to world. I mean "world" in the sense that Paul Ricoeur does
when he says that the task of hermeneutics is to reveal the "desti-
nation of discourse as projecting a world," or when he says that
"for me, the world is the ensemble of references opened up by
every kind of text."[14] But when the ruins are all around the land,
as *you* can see; when *you* know how water can make foam, can
make suds; when *you* yourself have seen Nepayatamu and the
Molaawe at the kiva—I do not know whether the text is opening
up the world or the world is opening up the text. This problem is
written larger in the narrative as a whole. The world was *already
there*; we human beings, or "daylight people" as the Zunis call us,
were already there; and as the narrative details, there were already priesthoods and even a whole village down there in the Soot
Room, and the priesthoods were in possession of the seeds of every
kind of plant that would grow up here in this world. Still, it is
true, we were in the dark, and the world up here on this layer,
even if it already existed, had not yet been revealed to us. The Sun
Father gave his twin sons the *word* that we were to come out into
the daylight, and they brought that *word* down to the priests.
The priests responded by setting themselves the lengthy project of
getting us out into the daylight. It looks as though the discourse of
the Sun Father had, to paraphrase Ricoeur, projected a world for
us. Or if we follow Ricoeur's recent abandonment of the phenomenological concern with the author's intentions, the Word itself
projects a world for us. But "project" seems like the disembodied
ghost of the author's intention, the will of God working itself out
in the creation of the world. There is something too inevitable
about it all. The word in the Zuni beginning, the word brought
by the twin sons of the Sun Father, is *pewiyulhahna*, a word that
is *yulhahna*: *lha-* means important, or even *too* important, *too*

much; but the -*hna* on the end makes that negative and the *yu-* on the front puts the word in the indeterminative: *yulhahna*, "sort of not too important," or the word is of "indeterminate importance." It is a word of *some* importance, but perhaps not *too* much.

The Kyaklo text and the available priestly interpretations hint at a general theme of indeterminacy that goes beyond terminological questions, but Andrew's interpretation develops that theme fully. First of all, when the people from the first room emerge into this world, he does not even mention that the Sun Father played any role. When it comes to the second people, the Sun Father simply remarks, "Well, perhaps if the ones who live in the second room come out, it will be good." About the third people the narrator says, "Those who lived in the third room beneath were summoned"; if it was the Sun Father who summoned them, this is only implicit, but at least we have a glimpse of a will here. Now, we may think, the next stage will be to put the Sun Father and the will together. Here is the way it goes:

> The ones who were living in the fourth room
> were needed
>
> but
> the Sun was thinking
>
> he was thinking
> that he did not know what would happen now.

What does happen is the rain, the waterfall, and the sprouting of the twins from the foam. Then we are told, "Their father brought them to life," which points to the operation of will again, but the very next line simply says, "They came out of the suds," and we were previously told that they "sprouted." Whatever is at work here, or *not quite* at work, there is a meeting of the sunlight and the foam of the waterfall, and out come the twins. When the Sun Father tells the twins about the people of the fourth room, ourselves, he says:

> You will bring them out, and *perhaps then*
> as I have in mind
> they will offer me a prayer-meal.

"Perhaps," he says, perhaps. The twins say this:

> We will *try*.
> This place where they may or may not live is *far*
> There in the room full of *soot*.

When they enter the fourth room and find the village there, they meet up with a person who happens to be out hunting. This is their first meeting with the *moss people*, the people who are living in total darkness but are about to receive the Word of the Sun Father, the word that will project a world for them. This hunter they meet is a modest person; he speaks with a weak voice. But before they have explained their project, he remarks,

> Well, perhaps I
> might know why it is you came.

He takes them to the village, where they meet the Talking Priest, the Spokesman, and give him their "word of indeterminate importance" concerning emergence into the daylight. He responds:

> Indeed.

> But even if that is what you have in mind
> How will it be done?

And he even asks them directly, "*Do you have the means for getting out there* successfully?" To which they respond,

> *Well*
> well, no.

The Spokesman then suggests they call in the Priest of the North. But the Priest of the North does not know how to get out of the Soot Room and suggests the West Priest. The West Priest does not know and suggests the South Priest, and the South Priest suggests the East Priest, and the East Priest says, "I, least of *all*." He suggests the twins, who brought the word in the first place: "Perhaps they know how to do this after all," he says, and they say,

> Well
> Well *I don't know*.
> But I will *try* something.

The twins take all the people along toward the east for a distance and then go ahead of them a little. When they find themselves alone, one of them says to the other, "What are we going to do?" And the other makes a further suggestion, prefaced with a "perhaps." With just such questions and perhapses they manage to find a way up through the third, second, and first rooms. In each room they plant a tree, and the branches of that tree form a spiral staircase into the next and lighter room. But the seeds of all plants were already there in the dark, in the possession of the priests of the moss people.

When they are all in the first room beneath, where everything is the color of dawn, the twins·make an announcement to the people:[15]

> *Now you must step from branch to branch again*
> *until we come out, out into our Sun Father's daylight.*
>   *Even though it will be hard*
> *you must do your best*
> to look at your father
> for you will hardly be able to *see*
> There in the room full of soot, when we entered upon your
>   roads, we could hardly *see*.
> That is the way it will be with you, *certainly*.

So, just as the Ahayuuta could not see in the Soot Room, so the moss people will not be able to see in the daylight. This is the kind of thing that structural analysis is made of. But wait a minute: this is not a trade-off of opposites: "You will *hardly* be able to see," they say to the people, and they say of themselves in the Soot Room, "We could *hardly* see." The hunter they met there said, "Well, perhaps I might know why it is you came," and the twins, the sons of the Sun Father and the bearers of his Word, said they would *try* something. And when the people finally come out of the dawn room, they come out not at midday but at the same moment the sun *rises*. It is hard, but they *look at* their Sun Father. At daybreak.

Now the twins take the people eastward for some distance, the first step of a migration that will lead to the place where the town of Zuni now stands. The twins make an announcement:

"Now
we will stay here four days," they said. *They were going to
stay four years.*
For four years they lived where they had stopped.

So the twins say four *days*, but our narrator tells us they mean (or
the text means) four *years*. Kyaklo does not tell us this: it is *not* in
the *book*, but this particular detail is a part of *all interpretations*.
It is like the comment of a scholiast in an ancient written text, but
it has not become embedded in the text itself. At the same time it
is not set apart in a treatise on theology. It is not the subject of an
argument over whether the Book really means seven days. What
the Ahayuuta *say* is four *days*, and what they mean is four *years*.
But there is something more here than just an explanation, a sort
of translation, of the mysterious language of the Ahayuuta. We
cannot just say, "All right, they really mean four years," and be
done with it. It still remains that they *said* four *days*. And if we
look again, we see that our interpreter did not say they *meant*
four years. The Ahayuuta say, "We will stay here four days," and
the interpreter says, "They were going to stay four years." But
this is not a deviation from *plan*, either. After the four years are
up, the Ahayuuta say, "We've been here *four days*." But I don't
want to say, therefore, that they *meant* four years in some kind of
code language. When we decode that, we have nothing left. We
might as well erase "days" and replace it with "years." But our interpreter puts four days *alongside* four years, and in fact he does it
two different times, once at the opening of this episode and once
at the close, just in case we might miss it.

    Now, suppose we have heard an interpretation or two of
"that which was the beginning," and we finally have an opportunity to go and listen to Kyaklo. When we hear him saying "four
days," then we'll know. . . . What will we know? Whatever we
think, he *says* four days. But we cannot stop knowing about the
four years. Something is happening with time here, within time,
something with its marking and its duration, and it is happening
between the text and the interpretation. It seems like *ages*. It
seems like only *yesterday*.

    Who are these Ahayuuta, these twins, who talk like this?
Their name is a clue, because they both go by the same name—

Ahayuuta—whereas no two living people should ever have the same name. Once in a great while the Ahayuuta reveal, as they do elsewhere in the present narrative, that they also possess separate names of their own, but they are as close as they could possibly be to the rift between being the same person and a different person. The Kyaklo text and all the interpretations tell us that although they are twins, one of them is the elder and the other is the younger. Of course: twins are born one at a time. But they are as close to the rift of elder and younger as they could possibly be. They are called Ahayuuta *an papa*, "the Ahayuuta's elder brother," and Ahayuuta *an suwe*, "The Ahayuuta's younger brother." They are named by reference to each other. If I refer to the elder brother, I am in effect naming his younger brother "Ahayuuta" and then saying that Ahayuuta has an elder brother. If I refer to the younger brother, I am in effect naming his elder brother "Ahayuuta" and then saying that Ahayuuta has a younger brother. What is called Ahayuuta is between them.

Neither text nor previous interpretations tell us what stage of life these Ahayuuta are in, beyond the fact that they are not fully grown, but now that we can listen to the voice of a narrator as he speaks their lines, rather than merely reading a conventional alphabetic transcription, we hear that the younger one has a high voice that tends to crack.[16] In other words, the two of them are differentiated by the rift of adolescence, even though they were almost born simultaneously.

The twins make everything possible; they are, in Heidegger's terms, "the rift of difference" itself. That rift, he says, "makes the limpid brightness shine,"[17] and this is the time to say that the Ahayuuta carry weapons and that those weapons are lightning. This is their *brilliance*. The people say they are *ayyuchi'an aaho' 'i*, "extraordinary, amazing beings." The people say they are *pikwayin aaho' 'i*, "surpassing, miraculous beings." *Pikwayina* is the Zuni term for miracle; it means something like "pass through to the other side." If the rain comes through our roof, somehow, and a drop forms on the ceiling and falls, then *k'a pikwayi*, the rain has passed through to the other side. But the Ahayuuta say, "Extraordinary beings we are *not*." They are a little small for their age; they are dirty; they have lice in their hair. They sprouted from the alkaline foam of a muddy flash flood after a heavy rain.

But "their Sun Father brought them to life." Is this their point of *origin?* Is the *will* of the Sun Father the first cause of all differences? Did everything begin with his Word? But the world was already there, four rooms full of people, already there, these people who might already know something. The Sun Father wants the people to come out of the fourth room: he has a desire in the matter, but he *does not know*, altogether and in advance, what will happen in the meeting of his will with what already is. And from there the Ahayuuta are "given life." Or, they *sprout.* What does it mean to say this is their origin, their starting-point? The rain was not made; the earth was not made: they always already were. When we go beyond the Kyaklo text and its interpretations to the *tales* about the Ahayuuta, we again find something that is not in the *book*: in all of those tales the Ahayuuta live with their grandmother.[18] Not with their mother—that would be the waterfall, we may guess—but their mother's mother. They always already have a grandmother. And what is *her* name? She is simply called Ahayuuta *an hotta*, the Ahayuuta's grandmother. Of course. Grandmother of difference. She is the patroness of midwives. And what is her shining? The Sun Father gives daylight, and the Ahayuuta travel on lightning. Whenever the Zunis touch a glowing coal or a match to a cigarette, they say they are giving their grandmother a seat in the doorway.

So is *that* the starting of everything? Can we stop here, looking at the face of the Ahayuuta's grandmother? And what is that face? One side of her face is covered with ashes, and the other side is covered with soot. Ashes and fire are already there together. In the live coal the ashes and soot are not waiting to be projected by the fire. Elder and younger are already there. The Sun and the people are already there. Desire and possibility are already there. The word and the world are already there. The text and the interpretation are already there.

NOTES

1. For an explanation of the orthography used here see Dennis Tedlock, *Finding the Center: Narrative Poetry of the Zuni Indians*

(1972; reprint ed., Lincoln: University of Nebraska Press, 1978), pp. xxxiv–xxxv.

2. For a fuller discussion of the nonalphabetic features of the speaking (rather than chanting) voice see Dennis Tedlock, "On the Translation of Style in Oral Narrative," *Journal of American Folklore* 84 (1971): 114–133; "Oral History as Poetry," *Boundary 2* 3 (1975): 707–726.

3. "Raising it right up" is treated in full in Dennis Tedlock, "From Prayer to Reprimand," in *Language in Religious Practice*, ed. William J. Samarin (Rowley, Mass.: Newbury House, 1976), pp. 72–83.

4. The lines of text and translation quoted here are my own revisions of the version of Matilda Coxe Stevenson, "The Zuni Indians," *Annual Report of the Bureau of American Ethnology* 23 (1904): 72–89.

5. Ibid. This is not a complete version, but it gives a clear enough sense of the texture of the chant. For complete versions of other chants belonging to the same genre see Ruth L. Bunzel, "Zuni Ritual Poetry," *Annual Report of the Bureau of American Ethnology* 47 (1932): 710–776. My description of Kyaklo himself draws from Ruth L. Bunzel, "Zuni Katcinas," *Annual Report of the Bureau of American Ethnology* 47 (1932): 980–981, and from my own field notes dating from the period 1964–1972.

6. For a summary of Zuni religious organization see Dennis Tedlock, "Zuni Religion and World View," in *Handbook of North American Indians*, vol. 9, ed. Alfonso Ortiz (Washington: Smithsonian Institution, in press), chapter 49.

7. The version of the Priest of the East is given in Ruth L. Bunzel, "Zuni Origin Myths," *Annual Report of the Bureau of American Ethnology* 47 (1932): 549–602.

8. For an example of the weaving in of chance events see Tedlock, *Finding the Center*, pp. 258, 271.

9. Dell Hymes, "Discovering Oral Performance and Measured Verse in American Indian Narrative," *New Literary History* 8 (1977): 441.

10. See Tedlock, *Finding the Center*, pp. 225–298, for a full translation.

11. This essay was given as a talk on the third floor of the School of Theology building at Boston University. The Zunis themselves make the analogy between the stories of a building and those of the world. The priesthoods conduct their meditations in total darkness four rooms beneath the top surface of the main building of the town.

12. See Ruth Benedict, *Zuni Mythology*, Columbia University

Publications in Anthropology 21 (1935), 1: 255–261, for a summary of previous versions.

13. All the passages quoted hereafter are from Tedlock, *Finding the Center*, pp. 225–298. Each change of line indicates a definite but brief pause; pauses of two seconds or more are indicted by strophe breaks. In the passage quoted here "a——ll" is pronounced with a pro- longation of both the vowel and consonant.

14. Paul Ricoeur, *Interpretation Theory* (Fort Worth: Texas Christian University Press, 1976), pp. 36–37.

15. The italics here indicate a louder voice.

16. See Tedlock, *Finding the Center*, pp. 168, 177, 179.

17. Martin Heidegger, *Poetry, Language, Thought*, tr. Albert Hofstadter (New York: Harper and Row, 1975), pp. 202–205.

18. See Dennis Tedlock, "The Girl and the Protector," *Alcheringa* 1:1 (1975): 110–150, for a lengthy tale involving the Ahayuuta twins and their grandmother.

9

Myth and Miracle: Isis, Wisdom, and the Logos of John

HOWARD CLARK KEE

IN THE HELLENISTIC PERIOD, Isis, whose earlier mythic role was that of consort and rescuer of Osiris (god of the Nile and symbol of fertility of the land), assumed a universal significance as the embodiment of wisdom, as agent of cosmic order, and as savior of the needy. While the older myth of her recovery of the body of the slain Osiris and her restoration of him to life continued to be told, it was in her capacity as goddess of wisdom and as mystic healer of the blind and the ailing that she was revered throughout the Greco-Roman world and that her influence on both Judaism of the postexilic period and nascent Christianity is most readily apparent.

The world view of the ancient Egyptians regarded the universe as essentially static. In that culture the changelessness of the world characterized both the realms that we would differentiate as nature and society. The static condition of the cosmos was not viewed as regrettable, since only the changeless was ultimately significant.[1] Even the inevitable fact of the death of the successive rulers of Egypt was accounted for in terms of continuity and stability through the myth of Isis. According to that myth, Isis assumed the task of reassembling the body of Osiris the king, who had been slain and dismembered by his enemy, Typhon. Through sexual union with the corpse, Isis conceived Horus, the new king. Thus kingship was passed from Osiris to Horus, a process which was reenacted in the succession of each of the pharaohs of Egypt.

The divine power which transformed one of the several potential candidates for the post into a king worthy to rule was embodied in the mother-goddess, Isis.

As early as the First Dynasty (in the late fourth millennium B.C.) the Pharaoh refers to himself as "son of Isis."[2] This myth of Isis remained basically unchanged for millennia, as can be inferred from attestation stretching down through the documents of the New Kingdom (after 1500 B.C.) to Plutarch and Apuleius in the first and second centuries of our era. We shall see that her cult and her cosmic functions change, as well as the specifics of her relationship to her devotees; but the basic myth endures without significant modification. The newer roles and attributes of Isis are in part derived from non-Egyptian influences, but they are also affected by the transfer to Isis of the functions of other deities from within the Egyptian pantheon.

Sometimes associated with Osiris, more frequently with Re (or Re-Atum) are two other divinities, or personifications, whose roles in Egyptian theology have a direct bearing on our inquiry: these are Hu and Sia. In the early theology of Heliopolis they appear, apparently as sons of Re-Atum.[3] In the Book of the Dead (175.38–44) Re-Atum commends Osiris for the results of the creation of the cosmos. Re says:

How beautiful is this which thou hast done;
Nothing similar has happened.[4]

To which Osiris replies:

I made it as the word (*Hu*) of my mouth.
How beautiful is a king in whose mouth is the word (*Hu*).[5]

Similarly, in a text from Denderah, Sia is described as "the heart of Re," as is the case in a Leiden Papyrus, where Sia is the heart—and therefore the thought—of Re, while Hu is his lips—and thus the expression or creative word of Re.[6] As Ringgren has summarized it, "In mythological language, Hu and Sia are the first-begotten children of Re-Atum and his assistants in the creation of the world."

Two related aspects of the religion of ancient Egypt also have a bearing on our theme, especially on the development of wisdom in the Hellenistic period: these are the deities Ptah and Maat together with their respective roles. Everything that exists is said to come from the heart of Ptah, the earth-god: the utterance of his thought made each thing materialize. "Each thing was first a divine thought, then a divine word: every divine thing came into being through that which was thought by the heart and commanded by the tongue. And so all that exists is but the objectivated thought of the creator."[7] The Egyptians recognized a divine order, established at the time of creation; this order is evident in nature in the orderly phenomenal processes; it is manifest in society as justice; and it appears in human lives as truth. Maat *is* this order.[8] She is the embodiment of the powers immanent in the world by which ordered creation functions. As one of the pharaohs declares, "I have made bright the Maat (truth, justice, order) which [Re] loves."[9] Thus Maat expresses the belief that the universe is changeless;[10] accordingly, the king's power is absolute, but it is not arbitrary, since he is under obligation to be guided by Maat.[11] Although there is in Egyptian religion no denial that movement and change take place, it is only the pattern of recurrent change that is significant, and that is a manifestation of the life rhythms of the universe which went forth, complete and unchanging, from the hand—or should we say lips?—of the creator.[12] As absolute monarch over the universe, both socially and cosmically, the chief task of the son of Osiris and Isis is to drive out or forestall disorder, or put positively, to establish and maintain Maat.

So powerful is this devotion to order that as Henri Frankfort expressed it, the Egyptian gods seem captives within their own manifestations. They personify power, but they are not portrayed as persons. There is an absence of drama in the reports about them, even a lack of narrative sequence. The moral teachings are presented as miscellaneous sentences; there is no codification of the laws, such as one finds in Mesopotamian cultures and in ancient Israel. The utterance of the king, obedient to Maat, is sufficient rule.[13] The pervasive sense of justice as stability is articulated in the Instruction of the Vizier, Ptah-Hotep (from the Fifth Dynasty, about 2450 B.C.): "Justice is great and its appropriateness is lasting; it has not been disturbed since the time of him who made it, whereas there is punishment for him who passes over its laws."[14]

In Egypt, however, as early as the New Kingdom we can see that a more humane and personal role than those of Hu, Sia, or Maat is assigned to Isis, who receives credit for acts of compassion, restoration, and protection:

> Beneficent Isis, that protected her brother, that sought for him without wearying, that traversed the land mourning, and took no rest until she found him! She that afforded him shade with her feathers, and with her wings created air. She that cried aloud for joy and brought her brother to land. She that revived the faintness of the Weary One, that took in his seed and provided an heir. That suckled the child in solitude, the place where he was being unknown; that brought him, when he was strong, into the Hall of Geb.[15]

The distinctiveness of the Egyptian fondness for order and continuity is apparent when we look at a non-Egyptian Middle Eastern culture. The fundamentally different outlook is exemplified in the advice offered by the popular folk hero, Ahikar, whose wise sayings are widely attested in Mesopotamia in several languages. A late version of his pragmatic counsel is to be found in a fifth century B.C. copy from Elephantine Island in Upper Egypt (although the sayings, which are in Aramaic, must have originated in Syria or adjacent western Asia):

> Gaze not overmuch lest thy vision be dimmed.
> Be not too sweet lest they swallow thee;
> be not too bitter lest they spit thee out.[16]

The ground of action is here purely prudential; we are a world removed from the cosmic order of Maat. Still farther removed from the Egyptian confidence in the pharaonic maintenance of order is that of the Akkadian mythology, as for example the myth of Adapa and Etana, where, as G. S. Kirk has shown, it is the deities themselves who are responsible for the breakdown of the divinely established order; rectification comes only when they are confronted by a culture hero.[17]

Turning back to Egypt, it is probably not until the Hellenistic period that Isis both eclipses Maat and replaces her. In Dio-

dorus Siculus' *Library of History*, for example, Isis has taken over
the role of Maat. It is Isis who has established the agricultural
techniques and procedures by which humanity may be fed. She
has founded the human laws; she has wrought justice in the earth
and thereby warded off illegal violence and *hybris*.[18] Together
with Osiris, Isis regulates the entire universe, giving both nour-
ishment and increase to all things. It is Isis who sees to it that although the seasons are opposed to each other, they nevertheless
"complete the cycle of the year in fullest harmony."[19] Moreover,
since she survived Osiris, her power surpasses his. Diodorus reports her as having vowed never to marry another after Osiris'
death and as having reigned in his stead all her days with complete respect for the laws. She became, he says, the cause of more
and greater blessings to all men than any other person. It was or-
dained "that the queen should have greater power and honor
than the king."[20]

Throughout the Mediterranean world and beyond—from
the Red Sea to the Danube and from North Africa to the Taurus
Mountains, throughout Egypt, Greece, the Greek islands, and
the Ionian coast of Asia Minor—explorers ancient and modern
have found shrines erected in honor of Isis, several of which include inscriptions. One of these, said to be from Nysa in Arabia,[21]
is noted and quoted by Diodorus Siculus:

> I am Isis, the queen of every land,
> she who was instructed by Hermes;
> Whatever laws I have established,
> These no one is able to destroy.
> I am the eldest daughter of Cronos, the youngest of the gods.
> I am the wife and sister of Osiris, the king.
> I am she who first discovered fruit for mankind . . .

Diodorus notes that there was an inscription of Osiris as well but
that neither is fully legible because both have been partly destroyed by time.[22] He credits her with having learned from Her-
mes the harmony of the stars, of music, and of the human body,
as manifest in the skill of wrestling, and with having discovered
health-giving drugs[23] as well as being "greatly versed in the science of healing."[24] Thus she combines within herself the mastery

of the order of the universe and the ability to minister to human needs. As we shall see, this combination of roles—agent of order, agent of healing—was to be paradigmatic for subsequent religious developments.

Aware that skeptics might question the ability of the goddess to effect healings, Diodorus asserts:

> In proof of this . . . the Egyptians advance not lessons, as the Greeks do, but manifest facts (*praxeis*); for practically the entire world (*oikoumenē*) is their witness, in that it eagerly contributes to the honors of Isis because she manifests herself in healings. For, standing above the sick in her sleep, she gives them aid for their diseases and works remarkable cures upon such as submit themselves to her; and many who have been despaired of by their physicians because of the difficult nature of their malady are restored to health by her, while numbers who have altogether lost the use of their eyes or of some other part of the body, whenever they turn for help to the goddess, are restored to their previous condition.[25]

Before continuing our investigation of Isis as miracle-worker, it is important to note that her role as sustainer of cosmic order led to her being compared to or even identified with other goddesses of the Hellenistic world. R. E. Witt has observed, "There is no end to her devotees telling the praises of their mighty mistress, Isis, the name above every name: queenly as Hera, mystic and fructifying as Demeter, comely as Aphrodite, victorious as Athena, and pure as Artemis, she embraces within her the functions of all."[26] Testimony is borne to the importance of the cosmic savior function in other female deities as well by Aelius Aristides' ode to Athena (second century A.D.):

> She alone has the names of Achiever (*Ergonē*) and Providence, having assumed the appellations which indicate her as the savior of the whole order of things. . . . She it is who holds off our real and universal foes . . . giving each man the true sovereign victory . . . by which folly and lasciviousness and cowardice and disorderliness and factiousness

and insolence and contempt of the gods, and all other such things take their departure, whilst wisdom and temperance and courage and concord and orderliness and right conduct and honor, paid to the gods and given by the gods, enter in to take their place.[27]

The documents which offer similar praise to Isis as sustainer of order and bringer of health have come to be called by modern scholars "aretalogies," since they celebrate the powers, or virtues (*aretai*), of the goddess. In addition to those included in ancient works,[28] such as Diodorus Siculus, a considerable number of aretalogies have been published by modern epigraphists.[29] Similar accounts also appear in ancient romances, such as the story of Anthia and Habrokomes, the lovers. As the tale is told by Xenophon of Ephesus, Anthia journeyed from Ephesus to Memphis, where she offered thanks to Isis. With Habrokomes she also called at Isianic cult shrines in Rhodes, Tarsus, and Alexandria. By the powers of the goddess they were delivered from storms and catastrophes through miraculous intervention. The love between them was transmitted by lips alone, in imitation of the relationship of Isis to the dead Osiris.[30]

The Isis aretalogies as known from inscriptional evidence are regularly in three parts: the first part testifies to Isis' nature; the second describes her virtues and her benefactions in behalf of humanity at large; the third details her specific miraculous actions in response to her petitioner. Aretalogies are verbally diffuse, varied in the themes they include, flexible in case usage (hovering between nominative, vocative, and accusative) and in person (with shifts from third to first, or third to second).[31] So widely do the aretalogies vary that they can be grouped only by cultic function, not by a fixed literary form.[32]

Among the more recently published aretalogies are one from the Sarapaeum in Thessalonica and one from Maroneia in Thrace. The former describes how a certain Xenainetos of Opus, while away on a journey, had a dream instructing him to arrange for the introduction of the worship of Isis and Sarapis at Opus. He was told that the dream would be confirmed in a letter he would later receive. Subsequently he did receive a sealed letter, in which the instructions were confirmed. From Delos and elsewhere the term 'aretalogy' is linked with *oneirokritēs*, interpreter of dreams, thus indicating that Isis' miraculous actions in behalf of her suppliants are interpreted by functionaries connected with her shrines.[33]

The most recently available text from Maroneia begins its praises of Isis for her benefactions by reporting how, in her response to a petitioner's prayers, his eyesight has been restored.[34] At first he could see only the sun—presumably light and darkness; now, he declares, "I can see your world." And, he continues, "I am persuaded that you will be present with me in every way."[35] Placing in a larger context his joy over the solution of his personal problem, he notes that it is difficult to formulate the praises of Isis, since she has so many attributes and achievements. He credits her with the discovery of writing and of languages "in order that the human race might converse, not only husbands with wives, but all human beings with one another."[36]

In words that reflect the growing influence of the Stoic conception of natural law, he praises her for having established justice "for each of us, so that just as each is by nature equal with respect to death, so also we might face life on an equal basis."[37] Addressing her, he declares: "You gave laws; at first they were called ordinances (*thesmoi*). Thus cities are well-established, for they found, not that violence led to law, but that law brought freedom from violence. You made parents to be honored by children. Isis herself was concerned about them not merely as parents, but as though they were gods. So then grace is superlative when a goddess writes a law which is grounded on natural necessity."[38] In the final lines of the preserved text we read that Egypt was honored because of Isis' gracious decision to make her residence there, but that her sanctuary in Athens brought honor to the city, not only throughout Greece but in all of Europe, and it served as a sanctuary for the whole cosmos.[39] Isis is presented, therefore, as the figure through whom the order of the cosmos was established, by whom the personal needs of individuals can be met, for whom widespread respect and affection are already rising throughout the inhabited earth, and through whom the ultimate peace and unity of humankind can yet be achieved.

Similar sentiments are expressed in the familiar address to Isis uttered by Apuleius in his *Metamorphoses*, when he is about to be transformed by her beneficence from a braying, bumbling ass to an eloquent initiate into her mysteries. Addressing her by various names of female deities, and associating her with their beneficent functions, he calls upon her as light of the world and as source of all life to come to his aid: "I pray thee to end my great travail and misery and raise up my fallen hopes, and deliver me from the wretched fortune which too long time pursued me. Grant peace and rest, if it please thee, to my adversities, for I have endured enough labor and peril."[40] The goddess approaches him in a vision of the night and identifies herself as Queen Isis. She promises aid to him, urges him to be "ready and attentive to my commandment," to eat the sacred garland of roses, so that he might be transformed into his true self. Obedient to her commands, as is the priest, who was forewarned in a dream about the ass who would take part in the ceremonies, Apuleius eats the sacred food and is changed. In profound gratitude he addresses her as "Holy and blessed dame, the perpetual comfort of humankind, who by Thy bounty and grace nourishest all the world, and bearest a great affection to the adversities of the miserable as a loving mother." She is extolled as one who never rests from bestowing benefits on humankind, who puts away all storms and dangers from men's lives by stretching forth her right hand "whereby Thou dost unweave the inextricable and tangled web of fate, and appeasest the great tempests of fortune. . . ." He concludes his ode, "I will always keep Thy divine appearance in remembrance, and close the imagination of Thy most holy divinity within my breast."[41] What this eloquent and moving text shows us is that by the middle of the second century the figure of Isis had become the rallying point for a mystery cult. Her appeal lay in her alleged ability to cope with the deep anxieties and frustrations of human existence: inexorable fate, social ostracism, the storms of life (both literal and metaphorical), deformity, and disease. Isis offered a sense of order, of meaning, of concern, of compassion, of power—and for her devotees a sense of belonging.

Within the same period of time through which we have sketched the development of the cult of Isis in the Greco-Roman world, Wisdom was fulfilling a similar evolving role within Judaism. In his study of Wisdom in Israel Gerhard von Rad has observed that in a broad range of cultural settings experiential knowledge enables human beings to function in their sphere of life other than as complete strangers and thus to understand life as in some sense an ordered system. The knowledge derived from experience and observation does not gain its status on the basis of the individual but exercises "its binding claim only where it appears as the common possession of a nation or of a broad stratum within a nation."[42] In the case of each individual, personal experience calls the corporate wisdom into question, with the result that "the sphere of order in which man is invited to take refuge is at all times under a threat."[43] Von Rad offers the further generalization: "Every nation with a culture has devoted itself to the care and the literary cultivation of this experiential knowledge, and has carefully gathered its statements, especially in the form of sentence-type proverbs."[44] This cultural feature is evident throughout the ancient Near East and was present in ancient Israel at an earlier date than the neat evolutionary patterns of nineteenth-century biblical scholarship allowed for until theories about the *late* development of Israelite wisdom were upset by the discovery of direct correspondence between biblical and other Near Eastern texts of a sentential type.[45] As early as the time of the monarchy in Israel, that is, at the beginning of the first millennium B.C., a worldly, human, cause-and-effect factor is evident in certain strands of the wisdom tradition. But this does not create a dichotomy between faith and reason, since Israel sees human rationality and divine activity on the same plane: God is known through human experience, and there is no area of human endeavor beyond his control.[46] Only when human beings have right knowledge of God can they achieve right relationship with the objects of their perception.[47]

Tensions did arise, however, between regarding the laws as inherent in the created order (as the wisdom tradition assumed) and the laws given by direct divine revelation. Significantly, the wisdom tradition almost never refers to the specifics of the Pentateuch, however much it sings the praise of the Law. Even when it exults that wisdom has taken up residence in Jacob, through the

Laws given to Israel through Moses (Sirach 24), no detailed precepts are invoked; rather, wisdom is declared to have been created from the beginning, before the world (Sirach 24:9). In the traditions of Israel, or rather of Judaism as we move toward the Hellenistic age, Wisdom is personified, though not considered a divine hypostasis; she is created by God and assigned an eternal function within the created world. She is female (her name is conveniently feminine in both Hebrew and Greek), and her personification occasionally moves to an erotic level, perhaps under the impact of the Astarte cult in the eastern Mediterranean. Love of Wisdom is enjoined under erotic imagery in Proverbs 9 and in Wisdom of Solomon 8. In Proverbs she sends out her maidservants to entice men to enter her splendid house. Pseudo-Solomon writes concerning Wisdom, "I loved her and sought her from my youth up, and I undertook to make her my bride, and I fell in love with her beauty" (Wisdom 8:2). Indeed, God himself is said to love her (Wisdom 8:3). The imagery recalls, of course, Plato in the *Phaedrus* (228c) and the *Timaeus* (46d), where love (*erastēs*) of thought (*noūs*) and of knowledge (*epistēmē*) are urged. Especially in Wisdom 7 and 8, where Wisdom is depicted in detail, the author has drawn heavily and in eclectic fashion on classical and Hellenistic philosophy: from Plato and Aristotle, from the Stoics and the Peripatetics, from Epicurus, and from language that appears later in Plutarch but which must have been part of the common coin of earlier Hellenistic philosophy. Not only the metaphysical terms but the ethical language as well are thoroughly Greek-Hellenistic. In his study of the Wisdom of Solomon James Reese notes, for example, that the four cardinal virtues, which according to Wisdom 8:7 manifest justice, appear first in Plato and then are employed by the Stoic Chrysippus (third century B.C.). As Wisdom declares,

> If anyone loves justice, her (i.e., Wisdom's) labors are virtues: for she teaches self-control and understanding, uprightness and courage.[48]

The detailed evidence shows furthermore that the author of Wisdom of Solomon was trained in Greek rhetoric and therefore has little in common with the translators of the Septuagint, as he diverges significantly in style and in vocabulary when treating similar subjects.[49] In recounting the sacred history (Wisdom 10–11) the names of all the heroes of Israel's past are suppressed; Wisdom alone is given credit for everything that happened from the creation of Adam through the Exodus and the entrance into the land of Canaan. In overall style, in detailed content, and in technical vocabulary[50] the heart of the book, which Reese calls the Book of Wisdom proper (6:12–6; 6:21–10:21), reads like an Isis aretalogy. There are more than fifty detailed points of contact in crucial vocabulary and conceptions between the portrait of Wisdom in this book and that of Isis in the aretalogies.[51]

Aretalogy, though a relatively rare term, is actually used in another wisdom writing, Sirach 36:13. There it appears in a context which is linked with the other dimension of the role of Isis in Hellenistic religion: praise offered for miracles and benefactions in behalf of the oppressed. It is God himself, however, who is addressed in Sirach 36 with an appeal to perform signs and wonders (36:6) by which the enemies of the faithful may be defeated, the sanctuary in Jerusalem preserved, and Jerusalem filled with "aretalogies" glorifying the God of Israel. From this the writer turns back to wisdom instructions (36:18), but the point is made clear: the divine is manifest in human experience both as order and as special succour for those in need.

What has become of the older Isis myth in which the goddess appears as maintainer of the cycle of life? G.S. Kirk, who has sought to trace the role of myth in Greek culture, assumes that Homer and Hesiod represent in their different ways the end product of a long process of selection and reflection on myths. Accordingly Kirk thinks Hesiod embodies a rationalizing approach, with his personifications, allegory, speculations, and mixture of logic, loose associations, and shrewd observations.[52] It is Kirk's opinion, however, that it was not until the fourth century B.C. that, as he phrases it, *logos* replaces *mythos*.[53] From our observations, however, the pair are two aspects of a single reality for the Hellenistic mind. The concern for order, based on observation of natural process, is expressed in terms of *logos*, or rather *sophia*. The affective and existential concerns are voiced in terms of *mythos*, of which *sophia* is the heroine. Deity in Judaism and in the Isis cult is discernible both in the maintenance of cosmic order and in the ministrations to personal and corporate needs through sign and miracle.

When we turn to a third religious development in the Hellenistic world—that of early Christianity—is there any evidence of the intentional combination of *mythos* and *logos*, of divine order and divine action, in response to human need for wholeness, individually and corporately? The obvious place to look is the Gospel of John, the prologue of which links the *logos* with both the creation of the world and the divine action in human affairs (John 1:1; 1:14). Only in the prologue does John use the term *logos* in the absolute sense. This is the case whether we regard the prologue as ending at verse 13, verse 14, or verse 18. If we include at least through verse 14 in the prologue, then the role of the *logos* is developed in a consistent way, not only in the opening chapter but also throughout the whole of the Gospel. The themes present here are creation by the *logos*, divine self-revelation through the *logos*, and the transformation of those who receive the *logos*. The myth of the preexistent companion of God, through whom all things were made, who brings light of the knowledge of God to all humanity—at least potentially all humanity—who seeks and rewards those who respond in trust to the divine agent, pervades the whole of the prologue. The correspondence between John's *logos* and the revelatory function of both Isis and Wisdom is thus immediately apparent. But since the term *logos* in the absolute sense is limited to the prologue, what can be said of roles in the rest of John that may be analogous to those of Isis and Wisdom?

It should be noted parenthetically that the male gender of the *logos* and the maleness of Jesus are quite irrelevant in drawing parallels between the respective roles. Obviously the author of the Fourth Gospel cannot avoid the firm tradition that Jesus was male. He did not take the route of those second-century gnostics who portray Jesus and all true persons of faith as androgynous. What is important for John is *function*, not sex or gender.

Our search for a role as benefactor of humankind to be linked with the *logos* of John is complicated by the fact that some interpreters of John think he has arbitrarily juxtaposed two quite separate traditions: the miracle stories and the self-pronouncements contained in the "I am" sections of John, neither of which matches well, if at all, the narrative and sayings traditions included in the other Gospels. As a result, several scholars have posited the existence of separate sayings and miracle sources.[54] The problem with this approach, in my view, is that only by highly subjective criteria can the critic determine what to include in the miracle source. But are the two elements—*logos* and miracle—so incompatible that their origin must be attributed to two different sources or that they must be seen as somehow in tension with each other?

Early on in John's Gospel the reader is informed that the succession of signs is of great importance for the work as a whole when in 2:11 it is stated that this is the first of Jesus' signs. The second is mentioned in 4:54, and the group as a whole is commented on in 20:31. There we read that the miracles—or "signs"—are not merely acts of mercy but manifestations of Jesus' divine glory, although the meaning is apparent only to "his disciples." In every one of the signs a human need is met, individually or corporately: the changing of water into wine saves the host family from embarrassment by providing the guests with the best wine at the end of the wedding feast; the official's son benefits from his father's faith; the lame man at the pool is healed independently of the curative powers of the pool; the hungry are fed; the man born blind receives his sight; the grieving sisters and friends have Lazarus brought back to them from the dead. Perhaps the stilling of the storm is intended as a seventh sign; in any case, it serves as the occasion for Jesus' self-disclosure to the disciples, when he identifies himself as *ego eimi*, echoing the phrase of Isis and of Wisdom. Similarly, in 8:55 Jesus confronts the Jewish authorities with his claim to both priority and superiority to Abraham: "Before Abraham came into being, I am (*ego eimi*)." Are these clues that the signs tradition and the self-proclamations have a more integral relationship for John than mere editorial juxtaposition?

The use of the phrase 'I am' in John calls to mind, of course, the self-proclamations of Isis. Two of these self-declarations are directly linked with the signs performed by Jesus: "I am the bread of life" (6:35) and "I am the resurrection and the life" (11:25). The latter comes in the midst of the story of the raising of Lazarus. In both cases a response is called for from the faithful and a benefit is promised: to come to Jesus in faith is to be guaranteed freedom from hunger and thirst. This is later clarified to mean that Jesus, as the true bread which came down from God, offers life eternal to his followers. A similar promise is extended to those who trust Jesus as the resurrection and the life. Thus we can discern in John the interconnection among three elements that we have seen to be present in both the Isis and the Jewish wisdom traditions: divine self-disclosure; personal benefactions by the deity; emergence of a responsive community.

The communal aspects of participation in Jesus as founder and revealer of the children of God are made explicit in two other *ego eimi* sayings: "I am the Light of the world" (8:12) and "I am the door of the sheep" (10:7) or "I am the Good Shepherd" (10:11, 14). The images themselves are unambiguous: Jesus is the one who brings light to the faithful (as we have already observed in the prologue), and he rallies around himself the true flock of God (again stressing corporateness, as in the prologue). In these and in the other "I am" sayings that we have already noted, what is offered is more than wisdom in the sense of objective information: the light is to be followed; the bread is to be eaten; the flock is to be entered, so that the members of the flock may be nurtured.

More abstract, at least in the terminology itself, is the self-depiction of Jesus as "the way, the truth, the life" (14:6). What is here proffered is nothing less than access to God, designated as Father. Knowledge of Jesus makes possible and leads to knowledge of God. The basis of Jesus' relationship to God is obedience grounded in love (14:31), qualities which it is Jesus' mission to convey to the world, in a manner clearly reminiscent of the role of Wisdom.

The most clearly mystical of the *ego eimi* sayings appears in John 15: "I am the vine." It is followed by the declaration that the followers are the branches and that they have now the possibility of mystical union with Jesus and, through him, with God in love and obedience: "If you keep my commandments, you will abide in my love, just as I have kept the Father's commandments and abide in his love" (17:10). By this means, fullness of joy can be achieved (17:11). It is not surprising that the formerly-doubting, now contrite Thomas in the closing scene of John's Gospel[55] ex-

hibits a mood of grateful adoration that is paradigmatic for the
Christian community but is at the same time akin to that of Apuleius prostrate before Isis, "the holy and blessed lady," when
Thomas addresses Jesus as "My Lord and my God" in John 20.
Similarly, Jesus final prayer (John 17:1) to God to "glorify thy Son
in order that the Son might glorify thee" has a parallel in the Mag-
ical Papyrus addressed to Isis: "Glorify me as I have glorified the
name of thy Son, Horus."

We have seen that pious Jews, influenced by features of the
Hellenistic world in which they lived and sought to serve God,
drew upon both the rhetoric and the substance of contemporary
mythology, of popular philosophy, and of current religious aspirations in their attempt to adapt older tradition to the new cultural situation in which they found themselves. Formally, a central clue to the adaptive process in Hellenistic Judaism is the use
of the self-predication style. Substantively the existential yearn-
ings of the seekers are addressed in two different but complementary ways: First, anxiety is spoken to by the declarations about
the maintenance of cosmic order through God's agent, whether
Wisdom or Isis; and, second, the more immediate crises, whether
personal or corporate, are ministered to by acts of intervention,
or special manifestations of providential concern. What is created, therefore, is a community of the knowing and the blessed
who both celebrate the order and rejoice in the benefactions accomplished through the divine mediator.

Both the religious needs of the Greco-Roman world and the
popular modes of meeting those needs have clearly and deeply affected the author of the Gospel of John. The miracle stories are
reminiscent of the Isis aretalogies. The self-pronouncements recall her self-revelatory utterances. The location of the entire redemptive scheme in the context of a creation myth—in which the
same agent comes from God, is the instrument both for creating
and sustaining the world, and also approaches humanity with an
invitation to mystical communion—is a basic feature shared by
all three of these literatures.

Thus between Isis and Wisdom, as well as between both of
them and John, there have been significant modifications of similar features. Theological predispositions have guaranteed those

differences, with the result that the distinctive features of John, as over against Isis of Jewish wisdom portrayals, are very real. In spite of mythological and speculative language John seeks to portray Jesus as a human being, with known human parents of both sexes (John 1:45; 2:1), subject to fully human limitations, such as thirst (4:7), weariness (4:6), and tears (11:35), human in his responses in spite of a foreknowledge of his fate (18:4). Most significantly, John describes the death of Jesus in such a way that no doubt remains in the mind of the reader that he actually died: it is confirmed by the soldiers and guaranteed by their piercing his side, from which flowed water and blood (19:33–34). These details are essential, after all, to document John's representation of Jesus as the *logos* become *flesh*, that is, as fully human (John 1:14). The death and resurrection of Jesus are presented by John as the avenue to eternal life, not as the guarantee of cyclic fertility, as in the death of Osiris and his resuscitation by Isis. The differences are apparent in detail as well: the grace of Isis has its ultimate expression in law grounded in necessity, as we have noted; but according to John the law, given through Moses, is now supplanted by grace and truth which have come into being through Jesus Christ (1:17).

Yet the agreement among the Isis, the Wisdom, and the Johannine traditions in the posing of religious issues is the more striking: there can be no mistaking that when John prepared his brilliant portrait of Jesus as the Word of God become human, as the *logos* made flesh, he understood the intellectual and religious aspirations of humanity, not in some timeless, universal terms, but in the language and conceptuality of the Greco-Roman world. It is the mythic language of divine disclosure embodying paradoxical love of both order and miracle that provides the framework in which John offers us his Logos.

NOTES

1. Henri Frankfort, *Ancient Egyptian Religion* (New York: Harper and Row, 1948, 1961), p. vii.

2. Ibid., pp. 6–7.

3. Helmer Ringgren, *Word and Wisdom* (Lund: H. Ohlsson, 1947), p. ii.

4. Ibid., p. 12.

5. Ibid., p. 21.

6. Ibid., p. 13.

7. Frankfort, *Ancient Egyptian Religion*, p. 23.

8. Ibid., p. 63.

9. Ibid., pp. 54–55. Cf. Gerhard von Rad, *Wisdom in Israel* (Nashville: Abingdon Press, 1972), pp. 69–73.

10. Frankfort, *Ancient Egyptian Religion*, p. 64.

11. Ibid., p. 43.

12. Ibid., p. 49.

13. Ibid., p. 135.

14. J. B. Pritchard, ed., *Ancient Near East* (Princeton: Princeton University Press, 1958, 1969), p. 234.

15. Frankfort, *Ancient Egyptian Religion*, p. 130.

16. Pritchard, *Ancient Near East*, saying tr. H. L. Ginzberg, p. 248.

17. G. S. Kirk, *Myth: Its Meaning and Function in Ancient and Other Cultures* (Cambridge: At the University Press and Riverside: University of California Press, 1971), p. 130–131.

18. Diodorus Siculus I. 14.1–3. Cf. Burton L. Mack, *Logos und Sophia: Untersuchungen zur Weisheitstheologie im Hellenistischen Jüdentum* (Göttingen: Vandenhoek und Ruprecht, 1973), pp. 35–40.

19. Diodorus Siculus I. 11.5.

20. Diodorus Siculus I. 27.1–2.

21. Dieter Müller, "Ägypten und die griechischen Isis-Aretalogien," *Abhandlungen der sächsischen Akademie* 53 (1961): 12–14. Müller notes that Nysa in Arabia is an unknown place, that the text probably conforms to an archetype from Memphis, and that Diodorus may have derived the provenance from a misreading of the inscription in which he mistook the last syllables of "Dionysus" for "Nysa."

22. Diodorus Siculus I. 27.4–6.

23. Diodorus Siculus I. 16.1

24. Diodorus Siculus I. 25.2–7.

25. Idem.

26. R. E. Witt, *Isis in the Greco-Roman World* (Ithaca: Cornell University Press, 1971), p. 110.

27. Aelius Aristides, from *Oratio II*, in "Praises of Athena," tr. Edwyn Bevan, *Later Greek Religion* (microfilm ed., Ann Arbor: University Microfilms, 1970).

28. For example, A. Festugière and A. D. Nock, eds., *Corpus Hermeticum*. Most inscriptions through 1969 available in V. Longo, *Aretalogie nel Mondo Greco*, vol. 1, *Epigraphi e Papiri*, 1969.

29. Listed in James Reese, *Hellenistic Influence on the Book of Wisdom*, Analecta Biblica 41 (Rome: Pontifical Biblical Institute, 1970), pp. 42–43. Albert Henrichs has proposed that "the spiritual father of the Isis aretalogies" was Prodicus, the fifth-fourth century sophist. His essay, "The Sophists and Hellenistic Religion," is to appear in 1981 (Budapest) in the Proceedings of the VIIth Congress of the International Federation of the Societies of Classical Studies.

30. From R. Merkelbach, *Roman und Mysterium in Antike* (Berlin: C. H. Beck, 1962).

31. Witt, *Isis*, p. 105.

32. W. Aly in Pauly-Wissowa, *Real-Enzyklopädie*, suppl. 6 (1935), p. 13f.

33. R. Merkelbach, "Zwei Texte aus dem Sarapeum zu Thessalonika," *Zeitschrift für Papyrologie und Epigraphik* 10 (1973): 45–54.

34. Yves Grandjean, *Une Nouvelle Arétalogie d'Isis à Maronée* (Leiden: Brill, 1975), pp. 17–18.

35. Ibid., lines 4–10.

36. Ibid., lines 22–24, 26–28.

37. Ibid., lines 24–26.

38. Ibid., lines 29–34.

39. Ibid., lines 34–41.

40. Apuleius, *Metamorphoses*, XI. 2.

41. Ibid., XI. 25.

42. Von Rad, *Wisdom in Israel*, p. 3.

43. Ibid., p. 4.

44. Ibid., p. 4.

45. Ibid., p. 9.

46. Ibid., pp. 61–63.

47. Ibid., pp. 67–68.

48. James M. Reese, *Hellenistic Influence*, has summarized the religious, philosophical, ethical, and anthropological vocabulary of the Wisdom of Solomon, and has thereby documented in detail the links between that work and philosophy, both Greek and Hellenistic, pp. 6–25.

49. Ibid., p. 31.

50. Ibid., p. 46.

51. Ibid., pp. 46–49.

52. G. S. Kirk, *Myth: Its Meaning and Function*, p. 241.

53. Ibid., p. 249.

54. The classic statement of this position in Rudolf Bultmann, *Gospel of John* (Philadelphia: Westminster Press, 1971), passim. See the critique by Dwight M. Smith, *Composition and Order of the Fourth Gospel* (New Haven: Yale University Press, 1965). More recently this hypothesis has been developed in detail by Robert T. Fortna, *The Gospel of Signs: A Reconstruction of the Narrative Source Underlying the Fourth Gospel* (Cambridge: At the University Press, 1965), pp. 38-44. Criticism of source theories for John in W. G. Kümmel, *Introduction to the New Testament* (Nashville: Abingdon, 1975), pp. 200-217.

55. John 20:26-29, omitting the epilogue in John 21.

10

The Myths of Plato

J. N. FINDLAY

I SHALL BEGIN THIS PAPER by saying that in my view the so-called Myths of Plato are themselves a myth and that what are called his myths really represent, with some decorative devices, a very serious ontology, cosmology, rational psychology, and theology which we moderns would do well to take seriously, since they may very well be true. The notion that Plato's accounts of reminiscence in the *Meno* and *Phaedo*, of the soul's mystical ascent in the *Phaedrus*, *Symposium*, and *Republic*, of afterlife conditions in the *Phaedo*, *Gorgias*, *Republic*, and elsewhere, and of the creation of souls and the cosmos in the *Timaeus*, are all to be regarded as allegorical stories, whose true sense is to be sought in this-world experiences and aspirations—all this represents the view of determined Cave-dwellers, content with Cave-phenomena, Cave-discourse, and Cave-science, and so incapable of understanding Plato, who believes we can only understand the arrangements of Cave-life by seeing them in the light of what lies beyond them. If one regards philosophy as an attempt merely to clarify, and perhaps slightly to integrate and simplify, the categories and principles that one follows in ordinary talk and life, most of Plato's thought becomes a bad piece of mythology, one which turns abstracted meanings into substantial entities, regulative aspirations into explanations, and dim presumptions guiding our inconstant, troubled rationality into beautiful, inaccessible fixtures that absolutely are. To such philosophers of the Cave the most valuable Plato is to be found in those early dialogues which record the brilliant logic-chopping of Socrates and in such late di-

alogues as the *Theaetetus* and the *Sophist*, where there are few
excursions into the transcendental and where clarity and inconclusive rigor are the writer's main achievement. I have no wish to
denigrate these great monuments of Socratic analysis: Plato could
dally among the minutiae of exact argument and construct arguments as trivial and as inconclusive as anyone else. He is sometimes, as in the great dialogue *Parmenides*, as much playing
about with words as establishing transcendental conclusions. But
one is certainly not understanding any part of Plato's teaching if
one thinks of him as a Moore or an Austin talking Attic, and perhaps both making and correcting mistakes that the linguistic ana-
lysts made in the present century.

     Before going on to consider a few of the so-called myths in
the Platonic dialogues, I shall try to sketch the ontology, the cosmology, the psychology, and the theology of which I believe them
to be an expression. In doing so I shall simply presuppose the thesis I have previously argued[1]: that Plato taught an Unwritten
Doctrine in the Academy without making it crystal-clear just
what he meant by it; that this Unwritten Doctrine can be recon-
structed, though not with ease, from Aristotle's reports on Platonic teaching; that it rated rather as a vast, unfinished project
than as a finished doctrine; and that it had many affiliations with
Pythagorean number-theory. I believe that the Unwritten Teaching confronted Aristotle when he joined the Academy in 367 B.C.;
that he was, from the beginning, one of its most incisive critics, as
also of Plato's written doctrines; and that he devoted a vast
amount of energy, including two vanished treatises, to its refutation, which at least testifies to its importance for him in Platonic
teaching. My views on the Unwritten Teaching, which agree
with those of certain German scholars, are of course at variance
with those of Professor Harold Cherniss, which have until recently established something like an orthodoxy in this country. I
do not, however, think that many controversial minutiae of the
Unwritten Doctrines make a vast difference to the main outlines
of Platonic ontology and cosmology: they only show how these
are generally to be interpreted and how seriously and how systematically Plato had conceived them.

     Plato's doctrine involves, in the first place, an immense *in-*

version in our ordinary view of what is, an inversion which goes with a great conceptual, axiological, and, shall I say it, religious revolution. Our ordinary view of things has for its logical subject or subjects the particular things stationed around us, things that impose themselves on our senses and the senses of others, that are variously located in space and separated from one another by distances that change rapidly or slowly from moment to moment, that are often many of a kind, or many more or less alike, and which seem to be inclined to conform to certain clear-cut, formal types which lead us to apply the same name to them all, though some of them are such poor type-specimens that we may hesitate to do so. Our ordinary view also includes other persons or souls alongside ourselves with whom we have communications, who are particular beings as we are, and who, like ourselves, also have an unmanifest inner dimension of "thoughts" of which spoken words are the normal utterance. To this realm of particular things a host of determinations attaches, which are pinned down by the meaning of words that we clearly understand rather than by the particular things to which they are applied: familiar or unfamiliar qualities, relations simple and complex, types whether roughly generic or ideally precise, logical functions such as identity, difference, being, nonbeing, and such, axiological denominations, and so on. On the ordinary view all these items can be said to *be* only insofar as they cling to the changing particulars manifest around us, or less manifest within us, in a manner we cannot further elucidate. They are not part of the primary furniture of being, as are particular things themselves.

Now the essence of Platonism is that all this gets inverted. What primarily are, are not particular things, but the generic or specific natures or characters that they instantiate. These alone are ontically ontic, while their instances derive all that they are from their instantiation of them. And these ontically ontic generic or specific characters are as changeless as their instances are changeable and vanishing, and they are as epistemically and axiologically perfect as their instances deviate from perfection in illucidity or in badness. Our experience of understanding what it is to be something, and perfectly something, also takes precedence over our experience of imperfect, illucid instances of that something; and not only is this so, but we can see in the former the true source, the explanatory cause of the latter, it being part of what it is to be an ideal, generic type that it can be *present* in imperfect instances, and imperfectly *participated* in by them. I am not on this occasion going to argue for Plato's great inversion, the turn of the soul to what he would like to be a higher, truer vision, except to say that it stresses a side of our experience as fundamental as the side which acquaints us with particulars, and without which it would not be possible to have dealings with particulars at all. For, if vanishing, multiple particulars are the units of sense experience, generic types are the units for the intelligence, and it is only if the former units illustrate the latter that they can in any way be known or managed.

Platonism of course goes much further than believing in the prime reality of generic types. It believes them to be ordered in an immense type-hierarchy, some more specific, others more generic, and some on a level with one another; it also locates them in an advancing series of dimensions, the most simple being the discrete dimension of the natural numbers, the next being the continuous dimension of lines and their proportions, the next the dimension of plane figures, the next that of solids, while a last probably covered the possibilities of regular movement. There is reason to think that from this ordered hierarchy of ideal types all sensuous quality was to be banished: these belonged to the realm of instantiation, and their explanatory nature lay in the arithmetical, geometrical, and dynamic patterns which underlay them: read the *Timaeus* on these points. There is also reason to think, from what Aristotle tells us, that the type-hierarchy included nothing deviant, defective, unnatural, artificial, or fortuitous except insofar as, on a well-known Socratic principle, a knowledge of what is perfect necessarily implies a knowledge of all that might deviate from it, fall short of it, fortuitously combine it, or be poorly modeled upon it. The type-hierarchy further embodies two *Archai*, or principles, which are far more basic than it is and which derive from Pythagoras. The one is a principle of continuous quantity, capable of indefinite increase and decrease, and as such unprincipled and bad, but the necessary raw material of all that is good and well-formed. The other is a principle of definite limit, which disciplines the continuum and breaks it up into orderly units and unit-complexes and patterns, thereby generating, in a series of acts which are only in form successive, the natural numbers, the lines, the surfaces, the solids, and the regular sorts of movement. The second principle was called Unity of the *One* in the Unwritten Teachings, but it was called the Idea of Good in the *Republic*: it was the originative source of all the *Eide*, and through them the source of all their imperfect instances. In its profound simplicity the whole hierarchy of the *Eide* lay latent, and their whole extension was simply the spelling out of its power. But it was also the source of all the intellectual acts that apprehend the *Eide* and illuminate human souls. And I also think that among its primal offspring was an ideal intelligence which human souls imperfectly instantiate, the Very Knowledge itself spoken of in the *Phaedrus*, *Parmenides*, and elsewhere, and the fabricator, according to the *Timaeus*, of our very beautiful, but in many ways flawed, cosmos.

Platonism is not, however, solely a philosophy of what transcends instances; it is also a philosophy of the Cave and of Cave-inhabitants, of the instantial world. On the Platonic view the deviations from good form which are only implicit at the eidetic level become explicit in the realm of instances: we pass into a region of disorder, of mutual interference, of imperfect participation, of the chaotic forces which the forces of Mind and Idea never perfectly bring to heel. And in the instantial world are also those two great Nothings, the media of instantiation, which are, in their undisciplined form, essentially and irremediably bad. The one is the great Nothing of empty Space, the Nothing which allows a multiplication of cases without distinction of character and which also allows all those senseless clashes which such a multiplication must entail. The other is the great Nothing, or rather Vanishingness, of Becoming, which, while always trying to achieve stable being, never manages to do so. This great Nothing becomes edified into Time, an imperfect, changeable semblance of unchanging being, once some order and limit has been imposed upon it. But into this disorder is injected the saving presence of Soul, the presence capable of ascending to the ordered realm of the *Eide* and always dimly conscious of it, but also capable of descending into the disordered instantiations developing in

space and of imposing forms and numbers on them. Soul is a remarkable amphibian, half timelessly eidetic and intellectual, and
half instantial and sensuous. Through its permeation of bodies
the sense qualities come into being, being begotten of the impact
of external on internal bodily motions. In one major instance Soul
is cosmic and presides over the cosmos: Plato sees this as an orderly assemblage of circles revolving about a central earth. I like
this Soul which is all impersonal ratios and proportions, and I do
not doubt that it speaks through the artists and prophets, as well
as the scientists. But of course for us men it is the lesser souls that
are important, since we are among them. Plato believes with
Pythagoras that these should alternate between incarnation and
disincarnation, undergoing a steady process of chastening education, of which a considerable part occurs, not when the soul is incarnate, but in the discarnate phases between incarnations. Then
the freedom from the body is marked by a freedom from the com-
pulsions, but not from the expressive and aesthetic uses, of sense.
Discarnate life for Plato is peopled by as vivid a phantasmagoria
of things frightening and lovely as in the clairvoyant journeys of
such as Swedenborg and Dante. The Christian visions of Heaven
and Hell borrowed much from Platonic sources, but they added
the intellectual and moral senselessness of invariable endlessness
in time, whereas in Plato sojourns in Heaven or Hell normally
come to an end in further incarnation, and there is even a suggestion (*Phaedo*, 114 c) that we sometimes transcend Heaven altogether. People generally think of the cyclical eschatology taught
by Plato as being Indian or Eastern; it is important to realize that
in Pythagoras and Plato it may well be originally Western.

I want now to go on from this general sketch to consider
what are generally thought to be the myths of Plato. I begin with
the *Meno* where a slave-boy's ability after a few trials and errors
to construct a square twice the size of a given square is attributed
to his soul's preexistence and to its having been born many times
and having seen all things here and in the other world. Since everything in the world is akin, what the soul sees here will recall
some of the knowledge it has accumulated in its long preexistence
(*Meno* 81). This story is taken by Natorp to be a mythic reference
to a priori knowledge, a Kantian myth of which Plato had no cog-

nizance. I believe the *Meno* must be interpreted more straightforwardly: the soul in its long career has had much opportunity to
learn geometry and has also in its discarnate phases had the
chance of direct acquaintance with idealized instances of geometrical structures and their relationships. It is on this account that
the slave-boy is so ready to arrive at the solution of his problem.
The argument is of course not very strong, for why should the soul
not have an inherent capacity to ideate geometrical universals
and illustrate them mathematically, a capacity which has merely
been touched off by the drawing of sensible figures and questioning? I think it plain that preexistence and reminiscence have only
been brought in because Plato independently believes in them, as
parts of a vast cosmology in which an immensely gradual intellectual and moral education of the soul is conceived. Alternatively,
the whole argument may have been genuinely Socratic, for Socrates had Pythagorean associates and used their ideas semiseri-
ously. Socrates in the *Apology* imagines himself conducting dialectical inquiries into virtue when he is dead, and why should the
soul not similarly have done geometry prior to this life and seen
fanciful squares drawn on fanciful boards by disembodied school-
masters? This would at least explain why it now finds the exercise
so easy.

I turn from the *Meno* to the *Phaedo*, a dialogue regarding
which I have definite opinions. I believe that it is in the main a
sober record of the reasonings actually put forward by Socrates
on that last sublime day, and that Platonic additions have been
made to it in discernible places. On that last day the soul's immortality was demonstrated by a typical series of logic-chopping, Socratic arguments: from the generation of opposites by opposites
(opposites were always a Socratic obsession), from the strange ar-
rival at precise mathematical concepts from defective illustrations, from the incomposite nature of the soul based on its invisi-
bility, its indivisibility, and its magisterial authority over the
body, and from its being so essentially a principle of life that it
cannot be associated with life's opposite, death. The Socratic
character of the arguments also comes out in the repudiation of
the Pythagorean view of the soul as a bodiless harmony, a view
which would have appealed to Plato, and which is in fact the

view adopted in the *Timaeus*. Into this web of Socratic argument
the Platonic ontology of *Eide* is cunningly, but at a few points
clumsily, injected, it not being difficult, with a little effort, to see
where the seams lie.[2] But the importantly mythic part of the dialogue occurs at the end where Socrates is giving a Pythagorean account of the cosmos and of the destiny of the soul in it. Here we
are given a vision of the true Earth as it floats in the aether,
shaped like a regular dodecahedron, the most sacred of the Pythagorean solids, with its pentagonal sides shining in a variety of
lovely colors. Our earth is merely the derelict, polluted part of the
true Earth, a part which lies at the bottom of a sea of air and mist
and whose interior is filled by a number of dreadful rivers. The
surface of the true Earth is described in very glorious language,
comparable to the descriptions of Heaven in the Apocalypse or in
Swedenborg, or in such Buddhist writings as the *Gaṇḍavyūha*
and the *Avataṃsakasūtra*. There the disembodied philosophers
and the other saints of Platonism will be privileged to dwell until
they pass to levels of understanding and vision that transcend sensuous description. But the river regions and lake regions in the interior of the earth are places of purgation or permanent penance
for the wicked, and particularly for those who have ignored the
deep thread of identity binding soul to soul and so have been led
to inflict violence and wrong upon others. Only when they have
had such wrong turned upon themselves in suffering and have
asked and received forgiveness from their victims, can they proceed to happier regions, and in the case of some very wicked souls
this time is never. The picture is as glorious and as sombre as the
Christian picture, much of which may have been borrowed from
it, though with the addition of some arbitrary and vindictive features. I do not think that there is anything that deserves to be
called mythic about it—at least not in the negative sense that the
term 'mythic' is so frequently viewed. It is a sober attempt to
sketch the outline of those parts of our spiritual education which
lie outside of bodily incarnation, and there must be some such
parts if our spiritual education is to be completed at all. The demands of virtue and duty, and of the happiness that completes
them, are very plainly not such, as Kant was to stress centuries later, as can be fulfilled within the limits of this bodily life. Of

course, as Socrates says at the end of the narration (which may have actually been made not by Socrates but by one of the Theban disciples of Philolaus), no reasonable man will insist that the facts are just as stated. But to contend that this or something very like it is true is reasonable, since the soul is arguably imperishable and headed toward the perfection of virtue and knowledge.

Turning to another fairly early dialogue, the *Gorgias*, one has the description (523–7) of the naked state of the soul in the life to come, a state in which none of its crimes and perjuries, nor its secret virtues, can be hidden, and in which no doubt all sufferings of its victims, or happiness of its beneficiaries, will be clearly apparent. The spiritual nakedness described in the dialogue is plainly an essential character of the disembodied life. Within the cover of the senses the sufferings of wronged victims can be ignored, but in the naked spiritual state we shall suffer them as if they were our own, and our own ugly hatred will be likewise quite manifest. I do not envy the disembodied Himmler confronted by the naked anguish of his victims and himself revealed in his naked malevolence! The happy love of those whose spiritual nakedness reveals only beauty and virtue must likewise be considered, and this leads me on to the myth set forth in the *Phaedrus*.

Here we encounter the triadic Pythagorean psychology of Reason, Valor, and Desire, symbolized by the picture of a winged charioteer with two horses, one high-spirited but docile, the other vicious and hard to manage. There is nothing mythic in this, only as much myth as there is in the various *dramatis personae* of Freudian psychology. Plainly there are three such principles in the human psyche: one longsighted, cool, and evaluative; another hot and aggressive on behalf of the personal self; and a third concerned only to savor immediate, low-grade satisfactions. The charioteer takes part in an immense cavalcade, each cohort of which is led by a god. The cavalcade proceeds to a point in the upper heavens where there is a vision of True Knowledge and all the Virtues, and also of absolute Beauty and of the shapeless, colorless essence of true Being, which is probably not different from Beauty itself. This vision lasts during a whole revolution of the heavens, during which time all the blessed *Eide* parade before the souls. In the *Timaeus*, likewise, the World-Soul sees all the *Eide* in the course of a single diurnal revolution. Some of the souls keep their place in the cavalcade, but others, unable to control their unrulier horses, sink down, lose their wings, and suffer incarnation. The dialogue is mainly concerned to suggest that love, despite its carnal admixture, represents the soul's recognition of the beauty it once saw in the face and form of its divine leader and which it now sees dimly reflected in the face of some beloved friend. I think it an accidental feature of Greek society that these friends were mainly male. I do not think that this story is meant to be really mythic. Platonism and Pythagoreanism see the sensible world as imperfectly embodying a series of mathematical patterns: arithmetical, linear, planar, solid, dynamic, and spiritual, each involving additional dimensions to the last and being as much patterns of beauty and excellence as of intelligibility and true reality. In a phase of our psychic existence before we became involved with the senseless multiplicity of space, the transience of time, and the obscuring weight of our bodies, we enjoyed a perfect understanding of that axiological, ontological hierarchy, worked out, not in reasonings, but in a single comprehensive glance. Now the beauty of an attractive face, and even more the beauty of a congenial mind and character, brings to mind the ineffable riches of the patterned hierarchy yonder, nothing falling short of due proportion nor failing to maintain unity in expressive variety and so forth. When faced with such a conjunction of spiritual and bodily good form we experience passion which cannot be explained by what is visibly present: we are transcendental creatures and suffer transcendental transports from whatever suggests the pure hierarchy of being. I see nothing mythic and symbolic in all this, only a reference, sometimes a little figurative, to what Plato believed to be the geography of being and the soul's place within it.

The *Symposium* tells a similar story. I believe that the account of the Banquet and the speeches made at it is entirely historic and Socratic (we know how faithfully records of discourses and discussions were preserved), but with the advent of the mythical prophetess Diotima, Plato enters the scene and describes the ascent of the soul from the admiration of sensuous, bodily beauties, through the beauties of laws and institutions and the sciences, to the admiration of Beauty itself, the principle of Order and Good Form and Mathematical Proportion in everything. I do not think that there is anything mythic in this account. What Socrates or Plato is describing is a sort of *yoga* which proceeds systematically from the sensuously illustrative and individual to the poetic and generic, and which carries the vividness of the former over into the latter. For while it is not easy, it is undoubtedly possible to rise to a concentrated awareness of Beauty itself and to feel in it the vanished yet concentrated presence of the specific forms from which one has risen to it. Those who have never practiced this particular sort of eidetic yoga will make nothing of the exquisitely beautiful mysticism of *Symposium* 210 and 211, and even question whether anything more can be here than an exercise in unmystical "abstraction." They cannot conceive that Beauty itself may be infinitely more intense, multifarious, and in a sense "concrete" than any of the poor semblances that spring from it, and that it may, as it were, conflate in itself all the Italian cities one has ever seen, all the fine cadences one has ever heard, and all these in greater passion and purity and unity than anything that one has ever experienced. The same sort of yoga is depicted in the dialectical ascent described in the *Republic*, where the mind that has risen from the calculative procedures of the mathematical sciences to the pure Ideas of Number, Proportion, Figure, Motion, Intellection, and such then achieves a further ascent to the principle of Unity, Order, and Goodness specified in all these Ideas, and not as an effort in empty abstraction but in face-to-face encounter. The mind can then apply the simple austerities of its vision to the infinite complexities and distortions of instantial existence. The figure of the Cave is of course a figure, but it does not stand for a series of mental developments that would end up in a mathematics department or a philosophy department at M.I.T. It is as much religio-mystical as it is intellectual and analytic, and it is meant to terminate in a sort of *samādhi* or ecstasy which is certainly not practiced in mathematical or philosophical departments. It is meant to lead to that concentrated awareness of Unity-in-multiplicity, of the Good Definite overcoming the Bad Indefinite, an awareness which is the source of all coherence in science and order in society, and in default of which a man cannot be a ruler or leader in a Platonic state. The *Republic* also terminates in an eschatology. Er, the Pamphlian, wakes up from the pyre on which his body is about to be burnt and gives an account of his experience in the other, the disembodied world. It is very like the account in the *Phaedo* and involves the same conception of the disembodied life as an interim between incarnations, with perhaps an ultimate liberation from the need for incarnation. It must also involve that experience of Heaven and Hell which must necessarily arise when souls stand naked before one another and before the ultimate standards and experience in their own persons the benefits and services, or the evils and wrongs, that they have done to others, sometimes being consigned to those unending torments which Christianity awarded much more liberally. The sojourn in the upper world ends with a vision of the planetary system seen as turning on the spindle of Necessity, with Lachesis, Clotho, and Atropos singing as they weave the web of history. I do not believe any myth is intended here, only the picture of a spiritual education regularly alternating between embodiment and disembodiment and presided over by forces that sing since they are logically optimistic, forces believing that order and goodness must prevail in the end, no matter how much leeway may be given to disorder on the way. This last is also the lesson of the myth in the *Statesman*, where the world alternates between periods when the divine helmsman is at the tiller and periods when he allows the world to take its drifting course. The interesting picture of time running in reverse, with men born from the earth and dying in their cradles, is, of course, a fantasy, though a very exciting one, with some relevance to modern speculations about time-reversal, change in the direction of entropy, and so forth. But the notion that the bad or evil, in being excluded from the eidetically good, is also in a sense included in it—there is only *one* science of contraries—and that there are accordingly always possibilities of bad form and deviations from goodness in the realm of instances, is a profoundly valuable and illuminating idea. The existence of a world of instances logically demands *real* departures from perfection, which are merely implicit in the eidetic patterns which make up that perfection. Instances which never abuse this freedom to differ from their *Eide* would in fact not be instances. A world of monotonously recurrent, perfect instances differing from one another like the shrubs in some gardens would not really exhibit instantial variety: the recurrent instances would collapse into a single instance surrounded by countless mirror-images of itself. And there could, as Leibniz says, be no sufficient reason why such a meaningless self-mirroring should exist.

I turn finally to the *Timaeus*, the most mythically mythic (or supposedly so) of Plato's dialogues. Here we have the tale of a World-Fabricator or Artificer who is hard to find or declare, who makes neither the comprehensive, zoological pattern that he follows in his total fabrication nor the original disorder which he orders in terms of that pattern. Here we also have the creation of ordered Time going together with the creation of the regularly revolving heavens and heavenly bodies, and, together with Time, the creation of the cosmic Soul which is responsible for the unending heavenly movement. Here also we have the making of the Soul out of a blend of three prior blends, a blend of the eternal essence of the *Eide* and the changeable essence of sensible things, a blend of eternal identity with the identity of changeable things, and a blend of eternal difference with the differences of sensible instances. The blend of these blends enables the cosmic Soul, in its revolutions, to run through the whole gamut of the *Eide* as well as through the whole range of their instances. The Soul is also ironed out into a long strip and divided into sections which realize the first three powers of the Dyad and Triad; into these divisions are then intercalated, in a manner that had a strange appeal to Plato, other finer divisions which assimilate the Soul's structure to that of a rather curious musical scale. Aristotle tells us that Plato also structured the Soul in manners that mirror the Point, the Line, the Surface, and the Solid and which corresponded to the cognitive differences of Intuition, True Judgment, Opinion, and Sense Perception. The Soul thus structured was cut up into a number of circular strips, each responsible for the regular motion of a planet or starry system, a topic of great interest in the Academy. The cosmic Fabricator then made inferior souls on the same sort of recipe as the cosmic Soul, only with less pure ingredients: the souls thus constituted had bodies manufactured for them by inferior divinities and were liable to the same alterations of incarnation and disincarnation as in the other Platonic accounts. The geometric structure of the elementary bodies and their compounds is then gone into with much detail and with great ingenuity. Immense ingenuity is also expended on anatomy and physiology, on the theory of sense perception, of breathing, of circulation, of reproduction, and so forth. What does this whole story amount to?

It amounts to an assertion that the world instantiates a hierarchy of ordered patterns, in which the simpler arithmetical, geometrical, and dynamic patterns are subordinated to the purposive patterns of life. This ordered, timeless hierarchy is objective to an Intelligence which is itself eidetic and timeless but such that—with a kind of free self-giving, which is also after a fashion necessary— it cannot but flow over into instances, which it seeks perpetually to make as good as is compatible with their inevitably deviant, confusedly multiple and changeable, instantial status. The timelessly Good contains in itself the possibility of all such instances, and it cannot permit itself the *Phthonos*, the self-sufficient, divine Envy and Jealousy, which would prevent its abundance, its *Aphthonia*, from freely flowing forth into the realm of instances. It accordingly sets spherical bounds to the Space, which is no more than the empty possibility or *Room* for instances, and it also sets bounds of ordered recurrence to the disordered flux characteristic of the instance as such, and so creates Time, measured by the sempiternal motions of the heavens and of the various bodies in it. And it creates Soul as the great cosmic Animal which runs through all true thoughts and opinions, and which is a Thinker, a Theos, in the Judaeo-Christian sense of the word, and not a pure Thinkingness like the Divinity from which it springs. And it also creates finite souls which are an even more distorted image of its pure, embracing Thinkingness than the World-Soul, and which will have a chequered destiny according as they throw in their lot with the confused multiplicity of the instance or the ordered unity of the Idea. And the souls have built-in structures which enable them to cognize every species of ordered pattern and also to impose whatever they thus cognize on the multiple flux of instantiation. It seems to me that in all this Plato is simply giving us his ordered picture of the universe, which in its essential form remains acceptable, even if its empirical details may have to be much modified. Instead of a sempiternal, spherical, geocentric cosmos we may have to have a centerless, quasi-spherical cosmos emerging out of a Big Bang and collapsing after aeons into its original unity and simplicity, presumably only to explode once more after a long age of quiescence, a picture more reminiscent of the Indian *manvantaras* and *prālayas* than the cosmologies of the Greeks and the Hebrews. But in this modern schema there would be nothing to prevent an ordering Soul or a dynasty of ordering Souls looking after different regions and periods of the cosmos and shepherding the inferior souls through the alternations of incarnation and disincarnation as in Plato. Problems of burgeoning population mean that these souls cannot be confined to the earth but may well be switched back and forth from one part of the universe to another according as this suits the needs of their spiritual education.

I tried in fact in the Gifford Lectures I gave at St. Andrews in 1964–1966[3] to use the Platonic picture of the Cave as the basis of an eschatology and cosmology in which I still believe. This argues that we live, not, as it were, at the heart, but on the outer periphery of true being, and that our peripheral condition shows itself in the pervasive presence of philosophical problems that can be resolved not on the surface where we dwell, but only as we retreat inward to being's inmost core. I believe that the world of sense experience, and of the language in which we so happily talk about it, is not the paradigm of the intelligible that modern Cave-philosophers have tried to make of it, but that it is throughout riven with absurdities which will take us beyond it to what I have called the Center of Being. Everywhere it reveals an extraordinary mixture of utter relevance and profound collusion: like the members of a secret spy organization, everything in this world is at once wholly indifferent to everything else and yet engineers the most subtle correspondences and interchanges with everything else. Space, which is externality itself, and Time, which is sheer vanishing supersession, are nonetheless the most cohesively unifying of media, in which the most remote things have a bearing on one another and have this even when they have ceased to exist.

And everywhere there is the most astonishing deference of one cosmic phenomenon to another, and sometimes to one quasi-central
phenomenon: witness, for instance, the deference of all phenomena to the precedence of light, so that whatever happens to the
mass, velocity, length, and age of things, light will always out-
strip them in speed, to precisely the same extent. The cosmos is
arranged like some small German principality where everyone
pays homage to its Highness: *was je geschieht, muss Durchlaucht
immer die schnellste sein.* These absurdities are, however, small
when compared with the great absurdities of Life and Mind.
That material particles should so organize themselves that remote
intentional references should be mediated by them, and remote
goals pursued by them, is so utterly incredible that its very incred-
ibility seems to be the very reason for its being. And even more
absurd is the profound sympathetic entry of one conscious being
into the experiences of another, experiences that he can never
in this world literally share, so that he may even achieve that
profound unity with the experiences of another which, in the talk
of this world, is impossible. Happy marriages exist, and their
happiness perhaps springs, in part, from the fact that they are impossible.

What I think is the case is that everywhere in our experience
there is a tantalizing oneness-in-manyness, an interdependence in
independence, which, as Plato says, drags us toward being, to a
point where vanishing will vanish, where instantial multiplicity
will lose itself in the unifying type, where sensuousness will be
gathered up into pure gist, and where the deviant possibilities
that go with externality, flux, sensuousness, and multiplicity will
pass over into the utterly simple and the simply good. I do not
think that one must imagine oneself as ever living exclusively on
the outer crust of being. In the life of fantasy one moves away
from it: the sensuousness of fantasy has none of the unmodifiable
compulsiveness of outer sense, while remaining similarly *an-
schaulich.* In one's dreams one has a dream-body, with dream-
eyes and -ears and a dream-environment, all infinitely shifting: a
whole scene dissolves and is replaced by another, the identity of
things and persons changes from moment to moment, and all is
enlivened with flashes of genuine clairvoyance. One knows what

people are about to say before they say it; one knows who they are, and where one's interview is taking place; one is instantaneously transported from place to place without worrying about intervening obstacles. This, we may suppose, is how it will be in the lower reaches of liberated life, since the sensuousness with which we invest matter is a spiritual creation and owes only its compulsiveness to the bodily evironment. Dante and Swedenborg and the Eastern describers of *Sukhāvati* all concur in the vivid sensuousness of some regions of disembodied being. And there will no doubt be some regions of lust and nightmare, as well as of blessed spectacle and reunion, just as in our earthly dreams. But in the higher ranges of thought and meditation, even in this life, we rise not only above time and space but also above sensuousness: we have concentrated *Bewusstseinslagen* of pure gist which, in the disembodied state, will be much easier to sustain and operate with than they are in this present life, where we are always running up to and down from sensuous illustration. And in our higher experiences, even in this life, we can in germ experience that melting away of the bounds of persons, so that while each remains other, each becomes perspicuous to the other, and the other to each self. This perspicuity, this spiritual nakedness, will be carried much further in the upper zones of being and will put an end, at the very least, to that spiritual solipsism which we all know to be nonsense even down here. And with the melting of the bounds of persons will come, more significantly, the elimination of hatred and indifference and cruelty and all that is most lamentable and appalling down here. And as one draws much nearer to the Center, the separated lifelines which lead to it will draw closer and closer together and, in so doing, will leave less and less room for that deviance from the straight for which there is much room at the periphery. In the end there will be hardly any room for imperfection. We shall become an assembly of just persons made perfect, lovely, loving beings grouped around a Center from which we derive all we have and are. This Center is by some envisaged as a blessed final State, the Peace that is always to be found at the center of a whirling wheel, by others as a Norm of Correctness which inspires all right endeavour, by yet others as the Wisdom, Being, and Bliss of a purified Self, by yet others as the Unity from which all Forms and Numbers spring, and by some even as a blessed and consecrated Nothing. But by many devout persons it is, as Dante says, envisaged in our human effigy, in the guise of a person infinitely concerned with the illumination, the strengthening, and the moral education of each and all of us. I believe that all these figures have substance, though some more than others: they all express the geographical relations of the Center to the periphery of being. For the Center is rather like the pole of our earth: in it all lines of longitude come together; one faces all ways at once; nothing is far from anything else. It is even more remarkable than the geographical pole, for while the latter is far from other terrestrial points, the spiritual pole is, by a sort of fluxion, present in all world-lines and also on the periphery. I do not pride myself on being at all an original theologian: my theology is all to be found in Aquinas and Cusanus, in the *Vedānta* and the *Mahāyāna*, as well as in the writings of Plato and Plotinus. And I believe that it even accords with the great gulfs of difference and alienation on which some Judaeo-Christian-Islamic thinkers lay so much stress. For the more the absoluteness of Divinity is stressed, the less and less can it be ranged as an instance over against and exclusive of other things, and the more and more must it, being Perfection itself, embrace everything that everything else has or is.

Am I sure that Platonism, or one of its transliterations, is true? I, living on the periphery and in this Cave, can in no manner be sure. But it is part of the phenomenology of our Cave that it seems to be open-ended and to provide access to an upper world which transcends Cave-limitations. Even if there is no liberated life beyond the Cave, we still have, as morally, aesthetically, scientifically, and beneficiently concerned beings, to act and live in the light that seems to stream from the Cave's open end, a point made again and again by Kant in his ethical writings. We have to act *as if* we had an immortal soul to bring to perfection, and in perfection perhaps to transcend immortality, whether or not we shall ever have the chance to do so. I believe therefore that one has to remain an eschatologist, a believer in Last Things, and to believe that only in the light of such last things can one's doubts and philosophical difficulties finally be laid to rest. And it is for that reason that I am critical of Professor Gadamer writing that religion is indifferent to verification, that it does not care whether anything it believes in really ever happened or ever will happen. For I believe that the religious spirit, which is also the philosophical spirit, is infinitely willing to change its view of Last Things, to exchange a natural for a spiritual body (or vice versa), or bliss in *Svarga* for the unruffled emptiness of *Nirvāṇa*, and so on, but the Last Things it still must have in some shape. Nothing would be more infernal than to go on mythologizing and theologizing and philosophizing if types and shadows *never* had their ending, and the newer rite were *never* here.

NOTES

1. J. N. Findlay, *Plato: The Written and Unwritten Doctrines* (New York: Humanities Press, 1974) and *Plato and Platonism* (New York: Quadrangle Press, 1978).
2. These seams are discussed in my *Plato and Platonism*.
3. J. N. Findlay, *The Discipline of the Cave* (London: George Allen and Unwin, 1966), and idem, *The Transcendence of the Cave* (London: George Allen and Unwin, 1967).

Author Index

Subject Index